Praise

'Giorgia's Master The Change Maze is a powerful guide for navigating the human complexities of transformation. She reminds us that successful change goes far beyond strategy and structure—it's emotional, cultural and deeply personal. Her insights into leadership blind spots, resistance and communication gaps are essential for anyone leading change. Giorgia delivers a compelling case for empathy, adaptability and resilience as the real drivers of sustainable transformation. A must-read for today's leaders navigating constant evolution.'
— **Richard Letzelter**, CHRO, Acino Pharma

'Blending mindful awareness with robust research and real-world examples, this invaluable guide provides a data-driven pathway to organisational transformation that resonates at every level, from the executive suite to the frontline. Through a balanced mix of pragmatic tools and people-centric insights, readers can seamlessly navigate the journey from strategic vision to sustainable outcomes. By adopting a calm, measured approach and mitigating resistance, leaders embed resilience and shared purpose within their organisations. This powerful resource ensures businesses remain agile, focused and aligned in times of change. In essence, it's a blueprint for cultivating the capacity for unstoppable transformation in a rapidly shifting landscape.'
— **Simon Young**, Data Engineering Director, BT

'Easy-read, full of practical tips and insights. This book is a lot more than a "managing change guidebook", it encompasses elements of psychology, behaviours and case studies, and gets you to think about how you approach change.

'What I love the most is that it is centred around the individuals.

'In a nutshell, a practical guide to help you become a better manager and a change agent.

'A must read!'
— **Valerie Nizard**, VP Global Human Resources/CHRO

'*Master The Change Maze* resonated with the challenges I face at work. The content is insightful and practical, offering strategies that I can directly apply to improve my contributions during organisational change. The real-world examples are particularly valuable. They provide illustrations of successful and unsuccessful change management in action, bridging the gap between theory and practice and making the concepts more relatable and actionable. This book is an excellent resource for anyone looking to effectively navigate and influence change within their workplace.'
— **Claire Barker**, Product Information Director, Global Technology company

'*Master The Change Maze* is a rare gem that bridges the gap between behavioural science and practical leadership. Giorgia Prestento offers a compelling, evidence-based roadmap for navigating the emotional and cognitive complexities of change. A must-read for leaders who want to drive transformation with empathy, clarity and measurable impact.'
— **Dario Krpan**, PhD, Associate Professor in Behavioural Science, London School of Economics and Political Science

'In *Master The Change Maze*, Giorgia provides an objective view and a pragmatic approach to change in complex, confusing and chaotic environments. As a specialist M&A technology advisor, it is evident that change is inevitable and constant, even when you are not aware of it or expecting it. The book highlights the diverse areas of impact; what to consider, potential gotchas, human dynamics, ownership and how to navigate all of that to ensure change is effective and deliver successful strategic outcomes. Even if the change isn't always easy, clean or according to expectation and plan.'
— **Jaco Vermeulen**, CTO at BML (specialist M&A Technology Advisory firm)

'*Master The Change Maze* is a compelling and practical guide for navigating change. Georgia blends strategic insight with real-world examples, making complex concepts accessible and actionable. Her emphasis on leadership, agility and innovation equips readers with tools to drive meaningful change in today's fast-paced business environment. The book's clear structure and engaging style make it suitable for both seasoned executives and emerging leaders. What sets it apart is Giorgia's authentic voice and deep understanding of human dynamics in transformation. Whether you're initiating change or managing it, this book offers a roadmap to sustainable success and resilient growth.'

— **Raphael Fainac**, CTO Apleona International

Master the Change Maze

A leader's guide to transformation without chaos

Giorgia Prestento

R^ethink

First published in Great Britain in 2025
by Rethink Press (www.rethinkpress.com)

Cover image © Shutterstock | Khaladok and
Venomous Vector

This is for you, Dad. Thank you for everything.
Saresti orgoglioso di questo libro, papá.

Contents

Introduction

Change is inevitable, success isn't. I have seen first-hand the challenges leaders experience when driving change in their organisations, similar to those you probably face today. Change can get messy and unpredictable, causes uncertainty and forces difficult decisions. Improving how we manage change is not just nice to do, it is essential for business survival and long-term growth. A well-planned and executed change saves money and sets the foundations for greater profitability. The good news is that you can achieve success by knowing what to look out for and having the tools to prevent – or quickly fix – problems before they happen.

We can look at change as a maze. We know our starting point and what we would like to achieve at the exit. At the start, there are many paths in front of us. We don't know which one is a dead end, and which takes us to the goal in the shorter route. Most of the time, there are twists and dead ends. At each junction, we have a choice to make. Change leaders use their expertise to evaluate options and select the most likely path to success.

Change is hard. Some research claims that most change initiatives fail to achieve their desired outcomes. Major infrastructure programmes, such as building a high-speed train line or digital access to healthcare information, are hit by delays and rises in costs, and many of them are quietly shelved. Even for projects that reach the finishing line, it's often hard to clearly see the benefits realised and the return on investment. Managing a change project can also be difficult at a personal level. Think of how many house renovations go over budget and are delayed, and dealing with builders is as challenging as with any stakeholder refusing to see your sensible customer requests.

At the heart of these failures, there is often a focus on the mechanics of change but a neglect in understanding human behaviours. The pressure is on to deliver results quickly, which translates into rushed decision-making, leaders struggling to build and maintain momentum, and, as a result, increasing resistance from employees. It can be harsh on both sides: a CEO being told of a major delay and presented with a request for more investment, or a programme director explaining the problems and asking for more time and money. Adverse consequences are not just about the company; one's professional reputation is at stake. Leaders are wise and know all of this. In the heat of the moment and with so many internal and external pressures, sometimes we tend to steam ahead and expect change will fix itself. It rarely happens.

Everybody nods along and agrees with Albert Einstein's quote, 'Insanity is doing the same thing over and over again and expecting different results.' Many companies keep doing the same things time and again and are surprised when they encounter the same issues. I don't claim to have a magic wand and the perfect solution; however, I know how to improve the way we manage change so we can achieve better results. My motivation is to see leaders optimise their approach to change.

My own change journey

Change management has been a long, winding journey for me. I got into it by chance, although with hindsight there were clues that made it a good fit. I always liked to make things better and got annoyed when things were done inefficiently, which made me a bit of a weird kid. I was also curious about people and why they behave like they do. Here is my story in three pivotal moments.

I stumbled into change management. A few years into my career, I started a job as a business improvement manager. I was not quite sure what it meant, but it seemed to be about fixing things, which I liked. One of my early projects was about improving customer experience, and saying that the team was not keen on the change is an understatement. They resented the situation and were not shy about telling me about it. Moreover, I was the young girl from HQ (I soon learnt that to be 'from HQ' is never a good look in any change). I didn't know how to 'do change', so I resorted to the common-sense approach of being friendly and listening to what people were telling me. To cut a long story short, it worked well enough, despite a rocky start. Some months after the project finished, I was back in that office and one of the most resistant employees told me, 'Thank you. I'd lost my enthusiasm for the job, but this new role has given me a new purpose.' Just like that, I was hooked. I loved the idea that I could improve people's experience at work and make businesses more efficient.

The second big moment in my change journey came sometime later. I was studying for an MBA, and there was a module titled – you guessed it – 'change management'. I had never come across that topic before. As I sat there at 9am on a Monday, listening to the professor talk, I realised: 'Wait a minute, this is what I do!' I was floored. People actually studied this stuff, wrote books and made careers out of it. Who knew? To me, it was just common sense – talking with people and listening, hopefully getting them to see things in an alternative way.

Now I knew that change management was a 'thing', I started learning and bringing theory and research to my previous trial-and-error approach. Even after studying change management, I found that the theories didn't quite answer my big question: 'Why don't people want to change?' The theories felt more like economic models than reflections of real human reactions. Something was missing from traditional models and theories, something I would spend the next few years trying to figure out. The answer emerged once I started getting into psychology and learning about behaviours. That got me to study for a master's in behavioural science; it is the third moment in my journey and why I am such a strong advocate of understanding the drivers and motivations of human behaviours to achieve sustainable change.

Who is this book for?

This book is written for leaders who are responsible for driving or sponsoring a change in their organisation; you may be in the C-suite, a transformation director, an HR executive or an operations lead. You may have the job of making change happen and want to lift the curtain and see the complexity behind the scenes. Whatever role you fulfil, business, technology, finance or HR expertise may not be enough to lead a successful

change. Same as in a maze, even the best-planned programmes can unravel in the messy world of change:
resistance, biases, emotions, misalignment and more.
Unravelling happens when human behaviours meet
organisational complexity.

I provide a roadmap that guides leaders through the
uncertainties of change, enabling them to learn from
other executives who forged their paths with creativity
and relentless curiosity. Leaders may be given responsibility for managing a significant change initiative
with little guidance on how to make it work. It could
be a digital transformation, integrating an acquisition,
restructuring or a major system implementation. No
matter what it is about, the reality is that it's different
to managing business-as-usual operations. Leading
change requires a blend of psychology and reliance
on data – and anything in between – as well as the
ability to navigate last-minute crises and unexpected
roadblocks.

This book guides you through the uncertainties
and difficult decisions in change programmes, as
well as providing techniques to approach them
with confidence and a sense of humour. You will
benefit from:

- Learning how to identify pitfalls and more
  frequent problems in a change programme
  so you can prevent them or solve them more
  quickly

- Ensuring the change initiative is tailored to your unique organisational culture – so much is about understanding human behaviours, from the board to the shop floor

- Designing the most appropriate measures, so you have the confidence that they will provide clear, quantifiable benefits

This book is not about providing a perfect one-size-fits-all solution. Instead, it's about empowering leaders with the knowledge and tools to improve how they manage change. Sometimes, it is a simple suggestion or an example that triggers a 'light bulb' moment with real benefits. This empowerment is what makes all the challenges and frustrations of change management worth it.

About this book

The book is structured in three parts, covering strategy and execution and providing a roadmap for leaders to navigate the uncertainties and difficult decisions common in many change situations.

It starts by setting the foundations for change, where leaders play the most active role. The first chapter focuses on strategic alignment. There is so much going on in a company that change projects can arise with limited connection with the strategic direction of the company. They solve a local problem but won't take the company towards its ultimate goal – sometimes they even detract from it. Chapter 2 is about identifying blind spots; there are recurrent issues that emerge in change programmes and if we know what to look out for, it's easier to solve them, saving time and money.

The second part revolves around people, because they are the make or break of a change. As a senior leader, you may not deal with specific issues directly; however, you need to make sure someone acts, and it is the best possible action. We often approach change from a rational perspective and aim to reduce costs and implement a new technology or strategy. Chapter 3 shows how people impacted by a change respond emotionally, which creates resistance. Chapter 4 gives an in-depth look at what drives emotional reactions through behavioural biases and assumptions. Chapter 5 is on the two facets of national and corporate culture – any programme needs to consider this context to succeed, be it a new operating model or mergers and acquisitions (M&A).

The final part is about making change happen, starting with changing our preconceived ideas on communications in Chapter 6. It may be considered the easy part, and we take it for granted, but it offers the most opportunity for improvement. Chapter 7 explores measures; despite our high regard for metrics, we need to be more careful in choosing the most useful data and be systematic in collecting and analysing it. Good data is the basis for leaders making good decisions. Chapter 8 is about developing a culture of continuous improvement, learning from mistakes and developing resilience. A resilient workforce that embraces change will keep the company innovating and progressing.

For more than twenty years I have worked beside senior executives, programme teams and frontline employees, helping to navigate the complexities of change and experiencing first-hand the triumphs and failures of transformations. I have also worked with technology teams overnight and on weekends as they were fixing last-minute glitches so we could be ready for go-live. I have seen perfectly planned strategies crumble due to poor execution, promising operating models collapse because of overlooked resistance, and costly systems fail to achieve the expected benefits. I have also seen the fantastic effects of engaging leaders, showing the vision and role modelling the change, and enthusing people to follow. In this book, I will share what I have learnt from managing numerous change programmes, including what works, what *may* work and what doesn't. I include examples in addition to stories from my own experiences to illustrate the theoretical points. Behavioural science and psychology pepper most of my thinking, but this is not an academic tome: it is a practical, no-nonsense guide to making change happen.

Change is inevitable, and managing it effectively is both a science and an art.

PART ONE

THE INVISIBLE THREATS: MISALIGNMENT AND LEADERSHIP BLIND SPOTS

ONE
The Trap Of Misalignment

M isalignment can sneak in at the start and at any time in a change programme, and it can take many different shapes: the scope may change, we may lose the balance between short-term and long-term goals, we may pursue an idea that looks good but will lead us somewhere else or there may be miscommunication. Many changes revolve around implementing technology, and there is often a discrepancy in priorities between business and technology goals. Businesses can also lose sight of the interdependence between day-to-day operations and strategy, or how departments fit together.

This chapter covers the sources of misalignment and why it happens. We also examine the hidden costs of misalignment and the ripple effect it has across the whole organisation, as well as the solutions. The impacts of misalignment can be pervasive and carry well beyond a single project. Employee perceptions and their experiences of change last over time. There is corporate memory in organisations: people remember a poorly run change programme or integrated acquisition, especially past redundancies. We will explore many stories and examples, before the chapter concludes with ideas and solutions to ensure much-needed alignment.

Asking questions to get solutions

Often, taking an alternative perspective is enough to pinpoint the root cause of misalignment, as we see from the following example:

EXAMPLE: Intel – it's all about the questions you ask

In 1985, business was tough for Intel. They had layoffs, their share price was rock-bottom and progress was stationary. In a conversation, the company's chairman, Andy Grove, and the CEO, Gordon Moore, discussed the situation while staring out the window at a Ferris wheel in the Great America amusement park.

Grove turned to Moore and asked, 'If we got kicked out and the board brought in a new CEO, what do you think he would do?'

Straightaway, Moore answered, 'He would get us out of memory.'

Grove's response was, 'Why shouldn't you and I walk out the door, come back and do it ourselves?'[1]

This example encapsulates the aims of this chapter. There is perfection in the simplicity of the question and the indisputable answer; the solution is evident if you ask the right question. The physical element of 'walk out the door and come back' impresses the importance of stepping away from a stagnant perspective and letting go of present and past constraints. Often, these are constraints we set on ourselves, and they are not serving us well.

The risk for misalignment is evident when planning and managing a change. Will the change align with the long-term strategy or may it take the company in an undesirable direction? I worked in programmes where the fundamental questions were not asked, causing them to fail or not achieve the desired outcomes. Leaders need to take a critical look at their businesses. If there is misalignment, they should ask themselves what actions they should take, or 'What do you think a new CEO or leader would do?' An external perspective is invaluable. Not everybody is able to

---

1   CS Sunstein and R Hastie, *Wiser: Getting beyond groupthink to make groups smarter* (Harvard Business Review Press, 2015), p. 114

challenge themselves the way Gordon and Andy did. Even in their case, it took them almost a year to pose the critical question.

The domino effect of misalignment: How it starts and spirals

Misalignment is never intentional. Instead, it is the undesired effect of some internal or external pressure. Due to optimism bias or pressure to make a decision, the change initiative may start without the necessary due diligence. The most frequent causes of misalignment are:

- **Short-term vs long-term.** A quick-fix change initiative is appealing when the pressure is on to deliver results fast. A short-term improvement can lead to a shift in direction or result in less funds for a more beneficial long-term solution. For example, a new customer relationship management (CRM) system may considerably improve how the sales pipeline is managed, but it will become quickly redundant once a more comprehensive system is implemented.

- **Local vs central.** I thought this was a problem only large organisations suffered, but then I started noticing it in smaller ones. Having multiple departments means people's attention is centred on their priorities. Although local initiatives and innovation should be encouraged, there must be a balance to avoid too much independence. For example, if the marketing department enthusiastically starts a campaign that doesn't align with forthcoming product features, this wastes resources and confuses customers.

- **Reactive vs proactive.** The pace of change is getting faster. Products we would not have imagined just a decade ago are thriving. AI has introduced even more disruption as well as opportunities for improvement. The temptation is to react to external changes: rushing the launch of a new product to keep up with a competitor or expanding in another country because everybody else is doing it. These reactive choices may not yield the best results.

Lack of alignment often comes to light too late. When it does, the situation is often not solved effectively because the discussion becomes emotional. There are complex group dynamics and behaviours at play, as we will see in Chapter 4.

Misalignment was an understatement for the situation I was asked to untangle in a major telecom company, as I will reveal below.

My experience: Aligning projects and strategy through a funnel

A large organisation I worked with gave a lot of independence to its departments. The realisation that something was amiss came when two different billing systems were independently approved for development in two separate departments. As soon as the decisions became known to the board, they stopped them and called time. The situation had to be assessed to determine whether it was an isolated case or endemic. The fact-finding proved it was the latter. Some of the planned or live projects either solved the same problem, were in conflict with each other or were not in line with the strategy. The situation was also causing a bottleneck of resources, with employees expected to work on multiple projects simultaneously, feeling too stretched and unable to focus and give the best of their abilities.

The findings were presented to the board and it was apparent that the company was spending too much money and effort on ineffectual projects. The clearest impact was financial, with unnecessary and spiralling costs. The second major impact was the wrestling for the same scarce resources to support the projects. Last but not least, employees noticed leadership's poor decision-making causing reduced levels of trust. The solution was to set up a governance framework, which we designed as a funnel: many project ideas could enter through the large side, but fewer would emerge on the other end.

It was a transformation in how the company had operated for a long time. We created a standard format for scoping ideas, preparing business cases, and mandatory financial information to be included. This objective was to achieve transparency and give senior executives valuable data to compare projects and make accurate decisions. There were five central departments, ranging from technology to operations, and each was asked to start planning and assessing ideas (new products, services and projects) using the same procedure.

The first step was to test the standard format. We unearthed all the planned and live projects (it was a bit like being a private investigator: nobody was quite sure what they were for and who approved them). We decided to apply the framework retrospectively. It may seem a waste of time to do so on live projects (and some people thought so at the time); however, it was a valuable exercise for two reasons: we could test our thinking and framework, and it also gave a clear message that the change was happening and was important.

We then started mapping projects and looking for any dependency or conflict between them. This was across all stages, from ideation to readiness. The focus was on ideation because stopping projects from entering the funnel was more straightforward. In the first round, we put two projects on hold but decided against stopping any in that initial phase; it would have alienated people and detracted support for the change.

Next, it was evaluation. Any project idea with a business case that stacked up, was aligned to the strategy and with neither dependency nor conflict would enter the funnel for the evaluation phase. The others were presented at a monthly steering committee of Department Directors, reporting to the CEO, who would make the decision. The decision had to be made at that meeting, without delays or 'let's talk about it next time.'

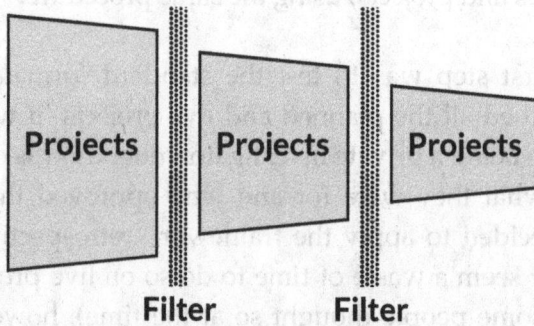

Filter as early as possible for better alignment; as ideas pass through a funnel, their number reduces.

How was the change received? The initial months were tough. People resented the change at all levels of the organisation: leaders saw it as a reproach on their autonomy (even if they were part of the steering committee), and managers resented the scrutiny and the need to comply with the guidelines. There was a lot of engagement and communication, emphasising the need for change and its benefits. Nevertheless, some managers complained when their ideas didn't go through the funnel or came to plead their case in the run-up to the steering committee decision.

I knew the tide was changing when (uninvited) people started joining the steering committee meeting, with an invite forwarded from others. Word was getting around that this was a cool meeting where people made decisions quickly based on good data. The original invite was not restricted; who would be so keen to attend a committee? It was not a party; we didn't even have cakes, let alone drinks! Although it was an ego boost, I soon restricted attendance. The decisions were shared openly and quickly after each meeting to keep people engaged. Over time, more people began to understand how they benefited from the new approach. They learnt the importance of writing a solid business case and gathering data, and were assured that good preparation made approval more likely.

The benefits of introducing the funnel were visibility, accountability and creating data-centric decision-making. The financial benefits were clear, with a high return on investment (ROI). It had a real impact on the organisation and changed people's behaviours; the company went from a hazy view of the pipeline and how it was spending money to having a good framework to align and optimise decisions.

When things go wrong: The hidden costs of misalignment

Wasted resources and additional costs

The impacts of misalignment are most visible in the wasted resources and additional costs they cause, which are relatively straightforward to quantify. The most pervasive consequences are the ripple effects of strategic misalignment on employees, market position and growth. That is why effort spent in planning can prevent re-scoping, modifying or terminating a project once it is in progress. Leaders prioritise exploring the opportunity cost of what could be achieved, diverting those resources to more strategically essential initiatives.

Poor customer experience

Equally important is customer experience and market position. No company is immune from messing up. A fast corrective action and a robust brand can recover, but this is not something you want to test. The following is a prime example.

EXAMPLE: Pepsi – how to quickly correct a mistake

In 2017, Pepsi released an advert featuring Kendall Jenner and portraying Pepsi as a symbol of unity. That was the year Black Lives Matter kick-started, as well as other social justice movements.

There was a quick and tough backlash on social media accusing Pepsi of exploiting a sensitive topic to promote a commercial product.[2] The marketing decision didn't consider the broader implications of the ad or what the customers' and market's reaction would be. There was a misalignment between departments and a focus on the short-term option of using events widely reported by the media.

The quick reaction from Pepsi to withdraw the ad within twenty-four hours and issue an apology saved it from worse consequences. Thanks to the swift public apology and the strength of a brand built over decades, Pepsi recovered. There was no long-term impact on the brand or damage to its financial performance.

This is a cautionary tale with a happy ending, but it's important to set this in the context of Pepsi being a company with a highly experienced marketing and branding team, which means this can happen to any-body else.

Lack of innovation and growth

The correlation between innovation and strategic direction is clear: innovation in the right products and services will increase revenues. Sometimes, the leadership takes their eyes off the ball and ignores what

2   D Victor, 'Pepsi Pulls Ad Accused of Trivializing Black Lives Matter', *The New York Times* (5 April 2017), www.nytimes.com/2017/04/05/business/kendall-jenner-pepsi-ad.html, accessed 25 April 2025

is happening in the broader market and emerging technologies.

The following example is Nokia, which achieved a remarkable transformation once but then failed to spot marketplace changes. When I started as a change manager, I often used this story as an example of reinvention and change – a prime case of leadership looking ahead, prepared to challenge its thinking. It may have been pride in its past achievements or a misalignment between the technology function and the strategic objectives, but, either way, it is an important lesson for all leaders.

EXAMPLE: Nokia – failing to spot a changing marketplace

In a snapshot, Nokia began as a logging company in 1865 and expanded in to paper production and rubber goods.[3] The real transformation began when it entered the telecom market in the 1960s, especially its move to producing mobile phones by the 1990s. It quickly became one of the dominant mobile phone manufacturers. Nokia took a leading market share by the 2000s with the Nokia 3310;[4] I still remember

---

3   Y Doz, 'The Strategic Decisions That Caused Nokia's Failure', INSEAD Knowledge (23 November 2017), https://knowledge. insead.edu/strategy/strategic-decisions-caused-nokias-failure, accessed 25 April 2025

4   D Lee, 'Nokia: The Rise and Fall of a Mobile Giant', *BBC News* (3 September 2013), www.bbc.co.uk/news/technology-23947212, accessed 7 April 2025

it fondly, virtually indestructible with a battery that seemed to last forever.

The misalignment started when Nokia failed to recognise the importance of emerging smartphone technology and continued relying on an ageing operating system. Even after Apple launched the iPhone in 2007, Nokia continued to prioritise hardware and underestimated the importance of software in the new smartphone, as well as the rise of apps. By the time it realised the shift in the market and tried to catch up, consumers were already enthralled by Apple iPhone, and later Android products. Nokia sold its mobile division to Microsoft in 2013.[5]

Nokia's story is a lesson on how easily even innovative companies can miss important shifts in the market. Its strength was hardware innovation and that department was driving decisions. That misalignment and pursuing the wrong strategic priorities led them to miss a critical shift in the market.

Lost employee morale and productivity

There is something I refer to as 'corporate memory': employees remember past events, and there may be stories from the past that are remembered and shared with newer employees. Because of how the human brain works, people remember painful memories more

---

5   'Microsoft to Buy Nokia's Mobile Phone Unit', *BBC News* (3 September 2013), www.bbc.co.uk/news/business-23940171, accessed 7 April 2025

vividly than pleasant ones, as the negative emotional imprint is stronger. This happens most frequently in M&As and reorganisations, especially when leading to redundancies. Trust plummets and is difficult to recover. The effect is a disconnect between employees and leadership, as well as suspicion towards any new change. I worked in a company where rumours of a change gave rise to what employees called 'conspiracy theories'.

Once lost, trust is difficult to recover, and it can impact organisations for a long time. Here are two cautionary tales.

EXAMPLE: British Airways – an erosion of trust

The culture at British Airways was employee friendly, with a focus on staff satisfaction and loyalty. There was a good customer experience and positive union relations. Under the leadership of CEO Willie Walsh, employee dissatisfaction rose after cost-cutting, redundancies and changes to pension schemes.[6] The lack of transparent communication and consideration for culture eroded trust and created friction among the workforce. This impacted both strategy alignment and financial performance.

---

6   C Boyle, 'Union Provides BA Staff With Link to Solicitors as Airline Brings in New Work Practices', *The Times* (16 November 2009), www.thetimes.com/travel/advice/union-provides-ba-staff-with-link-to-solicitors-as-airline-brings-in-new-work-practices-hdnbr6w3w9z, accessed 7 April 2025

EXAMPLE: Hewlett-Packard – layoffs lose moral

Hewlett-Packard had a collaborative and decentralised culture, which valued employee autonomy, respect and long-term thinking. CEO Carly Fiorina's decision to merge with Compaq was met with resistance from both shareholders and employees.[7] She went ahead, causing layoffs and decline in morale. Her autocratic leadership style was misaligned with the HP culture, eroding trust.

There is no judgement of these decisions; it is the role of a CEO to make difficult and sometimes unpopular choices. The lesson here is how the change is communicated and implemented, and that's within the control of the leadership team.

No company is immune from the occasional misalignment. It can't be eliminated completely, so the emphasis is on the capability to challenge new initiatives and planned changes. As we have seen, the impact of misalignment ripples in the long term and can lead to a company's demise. How can we ensure better alignment?

7   N Sekar, 'The Case of Hewlett-Packard and Compaq Merger: Building and Leading Teams', *Medium* (14 June 2024), https://medium.com/@nareshnavinash/the-case-of-hewlett-packard-and-compaq-merger-building-and-leading-teams-4bc3223b1d6b, accessed 7 April 2025

Proactive actions to achieve alignment

Awareness may be the first step towards making a positive change, but it is insufficient; it needs action. Leaders need to take proactive measures to ensure alignment across the organisation. Ironically, CEOs and others in leadership positions are best placed to have a holistic view of the company. However, the constant pull of competing priorities can blur that view and prevent them from achieving alignment. A leader can use their holistic perspective to create a culture that encourages managers to ensure their projects align with others, and with a long-term strategy. Once a misalignment emerges, a culture that's open to challenges ensures prompt corrective actions supported by governance. Alignment is not a one-off task; it must be reviewed as conditions evolve. A transformation leader once described a fast-paced, distressed situation where initial alignment was skipped to act quickly, only to later realise the lack of engagement. His mantra was to 'pause, reset and re-engage.'

Play it like chess

Alignment requires thinking several steps ahead when evaluating a change initiative and its possible impacts. We can visualise it as a chess game where we have to balance defending the organisation's core strategy (represented by the king), while seeking approval for a change project (the queen). While playing, we consider the different functions – or pawns – impacted by the change, as well as external factors: our opponent's moves.

In a workshop setting, this approach allows senior decision-makers to look at a situation from alternative perspectives. The need to think several moves ahead is becoming increasingly important; the level of complexity in any business – both internal and external – is increasing exponentially, so programme decisions must be considered as part of a wide ecosystem.

Use a governance structure

The culture described earlier requires a governance structure to facilitate those corrective actions and monitor progress, thus maintaining alignment over time. The story from my experience in this chapter exemplifies how the new governance model prevented disparate and conflicting projects from consuming resources.

Governance is sometimes seen as a blocker. Instead, it is the foundation that enables a business to be innovative. Once the basics of governance are in place, people can let their creativity loose. Any company with more than a handful of projects must keep track of them and report progress consistently, contributing the data leaders need to make decisions. Tracking progress ensures resources are allocated effectively, and costs are kept in check. Consistency allows comparison between projects and keeps you sane! I have seen the difference it made to a board's confidence level once we introduced a table that showed progress over time at a glance. Sometimes, the smallest things have the most impact.

Write down the answers

While the brain generates quick, automatic answers, shaping those thoughts into a clear, coherent explanation requires more deliberate effort. Depending on how we phrase a question, we get more or less useful information. Just notice how different the answers may be if I ask, 'Does this change support the long-term strategy?' Replying yes/no is quick and easy, but I don't get valuable information. If I ask, 'How does this change support the long-term strategy?', then I can't get away with just yes or no – I need to answer with depth. The goal is to achieve the most useful information. We need great questions to obtain meaningful answers. The power of the written word is about challenging ourselves to find better answers.

Start With Why, always

Part of knowing where you want to go is having a clear purpose and the book *Start With Why*[8] must be on every leader's bookshelf – or rather on their desk.

---

8   S Sinek, *Start With Why: The multi-million-copy bestselling management and leadership book to help you find success* (Penguin, 2011)

THE TRAP OF MISALIGNMENT

In this book, Simon Sinek explores how leaders inspire change by starting with a clear understanding of purpose. Many leaders focus on the wrong priorities of what to do and how to do it, but that's not enough to inspire loyalty and drive among employees.

Purpose is the driving force that brings all the different strands of change together, like an orchestra creating a symphony of diverse instruments. As we know from Martin Luther King's famous speech, having a purpose (or dream) is a powerful and inspiring message. This becomes the priority if the company's purpose is unclear or needs to be dusted down after not being looked at for a while. Once the 'why' is clear and owned by the leadership team, the scene is set to review new and live change programmes to ensure they are aligned.

Bridging the gap: Aligning business and technology priorities

A large share of business investment is in technology. There is no exact figure of global spend, but when you see some estimates hovering on $5 trillion, you realise how significant it is.[9] At the same time, many executives (88% of respondents, according to a PWC

---

9   M LoDolce and M Moran, 'Gartner Forecasts Worldwide IT Spending to Grow 9.8% in 2025', Gartner (21 January 2025), www.gartner.com/en/newsroom/press-releases/2025-01-21-gartner-forecasts-worldwide-it-spending-to-grow-9-point-8-percent-in-2025, accessed 25 April 2025

survey)[10] admit not achieving the expected ROI. Misalignment is a root cause in several major system implementations. There is a disconnect between what the business side wants to achieve and what the technology solution can provide. The challenge is finding the common ground and joining all the strands.

Aligning new technology with business strategy is essential for long-term success. The essentials are familiar: you need to have a 'why', engage stakeholders early, measure impact and – of course – invest in change management. I delve into other key components that don't get enough air space; bridging the gap between IT and the business is essential for any technology change. The following are key components we need to consider.

Developing a shared language

Every profession develops its own language, which is normal and necessary because it speeds up and improves communication. If you observe any group of lawyers or doctors, they talk quickly and fluently and know exactly what's been said. Once you introduce a client or patient to the conversation, their reaction is that the talk is unintelligible and full of

10 PWC, 'PwC Pulse Survey: Focused on Reinvention' (22 August 2023), www.pwc.com/us/en/library/pulse-survey/business-reinvention. html, accessed 25 April 2025

jargon, as well as scary and exclusive. It would be fair to guess that neither side enjoys the conversation. The same happens between business departments; there is a camaraderie inside each group that excludes others.

If you find yourself having to bring together individuals or teams across functions, the first advice is to be patient and draw out the similarities in concepts beyond words, one at a time. It's painstaking rather than fun, but essential.

This situation occurs at a senior level as well. I have been in technology pitches and supplier meetings, sitting on both sides. You can sense immediately when there is no shared language. I always encourage clients to request the language be set at the level that works for them (most of the time, excluding tech jargon) to understand if that's the right solution. Misunderstandings have the habit of growing bigger.

Beware of assumptions

Human beings believe others think like us, and these biases give rise to all sorts of assumptions. Because we are so convinced of our knowledge, we don't feel the need to check. As the next example illustrates, this is dangerous and can affect even the smartest people.

EXAMPLE: Mars Climate Orbiter – not asking the obvious questions

In the late 1990s, a team of engineers at NASA and another at Lockheed Martin in the US were working on the Mars Climate Orbiter mission to study the climate and surface of Mars. The Orbiter was launched in December 1998, and when it entered the Martian atmosphere, it exploded. It had a much lower altitude than planned and disintegrated due to atmospheric stress.

What caused it to explode? The two teams used different measurement systems. Lockheed Martin provided the data using the imperial system, and NASA's engineers assumed the data was in the metric system. This mismatch led to the incorrect calculation of trajectory adjustments. These were teams of smart people; however, they made an assumption and never thought of checking with the other team. The failure to convert units of measure led to a spacecraft exploding and the failure of a $327.6 million mission.[11]

This cautionary tale reminds us of the importance of asking basic questions, having consistent and frequent communication, as well as the need for a rigorous validation process, which means never making assumptions.

---

11 A Harish, 'When NASA Lost a Spacecraft Due to a Metric Math Mistake', *Simscale* (8 December 2023), www.simscale.com/blog/nasa-mars-climate-orbiter-metric, accessed 2 April 2025

Assumptions can sneak in at any time, so we must include regular checkpoints at all levels, from the chief information officer meeting the technology supplier to the implementation team on the ground. On the client side, assuming the new technology aligns with the strategy is the most dangerous.

Furthermore, this is not an alignment that's confirmed as a one-off; given the fast-moving environments we work in, both business needs and technology options available can rapidly change. Although I don't advocate significant changes halfway through a programme, there is the danger that the planned solution won't meet business needs, although tweaks may be enough to correct the path.

Shared objectives

The teams tasked with delivering the programme need to move in the same direction. We may expect this to happen naturally; however, their priorities are different. For example, a change manager's priority is to ensure high levels of adoption. The priority of process leads is to have the new processes clearly documented and shared, and that of the IT team is to install the technology. Although these are all components of success, the team can lose alignment over time if the correct dependencies and accountabilities are not in place. That's why the sponsor and programme manager roles are essential to provide direction and cohesion.

AI

Artificial intelligence (AI) is not a new concept. It has great potential to bring vast improvements but also to create great disruption, which raises important ethical questions. This is relevant to change because of the impact on people and organisational design.

AI is desperately seeking alignment as most AI conversations are technology-centric. I agree with many of the thought leaders in the field that we need to take a strategic and purpose-led perspective on AI. It is more than technology; it is about strategy, change, people and behaviours. More so than other new tech (because it is still relatively new), the first step is being clear about what problems you want to solve.

Summary

- Never make assumptions and step away from the current perspective. The solution is obvious if you ask the right questions.

- Misalignment arises from some kind of pressure. The three most frequent causes are: a short-term fix that doesn't align with the long-term strategic direction; conflict between local and central initiatives; and the temptation to be reactive rather than proactive, potentially deviating from the path.

- Misalignment has pervasive impacts. It causes wasted resources and additional costs and has ripple effects on customer experience, market position and growth, as well as employee morale and productivity. Recovering from a loss of trust from customers and employees is difficult; prevention is easier.

- Occasional misalignment can't be avoided, but the risk can be reduced by the capability to challenge new initiatives to ensure they are aligned with the long-term direction and prompt corrective actions. This can be achieved by thinking several steps ahead, having a reliable governance structure and giving leaders the data for accurate decision-making.

- Given the importance and size of technology investments, aligning their priorities with the business strategy is critical. Two components are often overlooked: developing a shared language and clear communications to ensure the proposed solutions truly meet the business needs.

- Assumptions can sneak in at any time and wreak havoc on the best plans, so always check. People and departments have different priorities, so setting up shared objectives can alleviate the risk of misalignment forming.

- The need for alignment is even more urgent in AI conversations, which are still too technology-centric. AI has the potential to disrupt organisations, and it needs to be aligned with the strategy and operating model.

TWO

Leadership Blind Spots: Hidden Disconnects Can Derail Success

We all have blind spots. They are most likely to happen when we let unconscious thoughts and emotions influence our behaviour. As a result, we lose impartiality and end up with negative outcomes. For example, making decisions under pressure relies on our brain's automatic system, when a fleeting moment can have vast unforeseen consequences.

Leaders are as likely to have blind spots as anybody else. Because blind spots arise from the unconscious, bias or lack of understanding, we can only recognise them with hindsight. It takes self-awareness and practice to prevent them. In this chapter, we will explore what blind spots are, their causes and impacts, and how to overcome them. The aim is to learn how to spot them in advance.

My experience: What I learnt from my blind spots

As an impatient person, I often don't understand why some activities should take such a long time to complete. This was more of a problem at the start of my career; I have now learnt to moderate my impatience, but it still occasionally surfaces.

There is one particular occasion when my bias towards action and quick solutions turned out to be a significant blind spot. My team was struggling with low morale due to a reorganisation and workload changes, so I jumped in to solve the issue quickly. I believed all they needed was an injection of motivation, so I introduced a set of initiatives: recognition for high performers and casual check-ins to build rapport. I went into this enthusiastically; if I was motivated, why wouldn't everybody else be? Once my changes were in place, I waited for the morale boost, feeling pleased with the speed of my actions.

After a month, a few employees seemed more upbeat; some showed slight improvement and others voiced frustration with the motivational initiatives. Something was wrong, and that was the shock I needed. I had to change my approach, so I slowed down, asked better questions and listened to their concerns. I learnt that the real issues were more complex than I had assumed. I discovered they wanted clarity on responsibilities, more significant support from leadership and opportunities for skill development. My mistake was to rush into action based on surface-level symptoms rather than assess the root cause of the team's low energy and engagement.

This experience taught me that a quick response, while making one feel better by taking (any) action and gaining a feeling of being in control, is a fallacy. To achieve a real impact and sustainable people-centred change, time, understanding and a willingness to explore beyond initial assumptions are required.

What you don't see can hurt you

A blind spot often occurs when our brain is on autopilot and assumptions and unconscious biases narrow our vision, influencing our decisions. A busy senior executive may not be aware of a key issue in the organisation, as they may be disconnected from the operational level and what's happening on the front line. The effect is missed opportunities, an inability to stop failures and – as covered in Chapter 1 – misalignment between strategy and execution.

If not told otherwise, executives naturally believe everything is going well, but there may be discontent and resistance as if it were a bubble about to

41

burst. Sometimes, either consciously or not, leaders signal a preference for good news, thus stopping some of the discontent and problems coming to the surface. This is a situation I experienced with the following client.

My experience: The case for good news only

It was a complex project, and one of the outcomes was people being made redundant or a fundamental change of their roles. It's never an easy situation, and being open and mindful of how people will react to the change is essential. Based on the information I was getting from employees and my previous experience, I knew it would be a bumpy ride.

When I joined, the programme had been running for some months already, and I was due to make the first of my fortnightly board updates since joining. I prepared my presentation, which included data on employees' experience and change risks; it was a compelling story for leaders to act. I presented the context, risks and my recommendations, emphasising the need to approach the change with caution.

Well, that didn't go down well at all! There was a lot of pushback and challenges about my interpretation of the employees' feedback and the doom scenario I described. It was one of my worst presentation experiences. I misread the audience: they didn't like challenges and messages that were not rosy. My bluntness was putting my position at risk.

The board had subconsciously developed information filtering. Their blind spot was assuming employees would react positively, or at least neutrally, to the change, so they expected the information presented to them to be filtered to meet their expectations.

After that first presentation, it took me time to develop a rapport with the board members through many individual meetings and lots of coffee. I learnt their drivers and wants and how to manage the blind spots of these executives (as well as my own!). I recovered from the situation by finding allies and relying on them to bounce off options, being better prepared for what reactions to expect from my updates. I could not overcome the barrier of unwelcome bad news, but I improved how I presented it. I balanced positives and realistic updates and made the presentations more interactive so that I could take them on the journey and they could draw their own conclusions, thus avoiding being the bearer of bad news.

In this case, the leadership was subconsciously creating a culture of sugarcoating. The overt messages were about openness to feedback from the workforce;

however, the covert message was that good news put the bearer in a better light.

When leaders miss the mark: Root causes

There are a few sources that may cause blind spots, so we will look at these now.

Information filtering

Information travels upwards through an organisation and communications may break down for several reasons. In my example above, the leaders' dislike of bad news caused negative information to be withheld or sugarcoated. Over time, this creates a hostile culture, causing actual damage by isolating leaders in an ivory tower. The result is that leaders won't know there is a problem, as no one is brave enough to tell them. They may even believe they encourage transparency and challenges, but their behaviours and the environment belie the reality. The filtered information can relate to operational issues, employee experience and customer feedback. Suppose customers are dissatisfied with the products and services, and the information doesn't travel upwards unfiltered. In that case, leaders may not get to know about it for weeks or months, making it increasingly difficult to act. This blind spot touches on corporate culture, which will be covered in more depth in Chapter 5.

Over-reliance on data

Data is the holy grail, but it needs to be useful, which means accurate and relevant. I have attended many meetings with brilliant-looking dashboards and reports, but when I ask about the data sources, I get a funny look from the presenter. If I ask how the data has been interpreted, the look morphs into dislike. The primary role of leaders is to make decisions; data gives certainty in an uncertain world, but trusting the wrong data is dangerous.

It is also important to interpret and get to the true story data tells us. To paraphrase the quote from Brené Brown, 'Stories are just data with a soul.' We need to go beyond the numbers, seek the context and capture the human side. In a change project, this means ensuring we don't miss emotional resistance, misalignment and morale.

I was consulting an energy company where the introduction of a new software was resisted. The leadership had followed change best practice and completed all the actions – or so they thought. I organised a 'reverse town hall' where the employees were the speakers and the executives were the audience. It was a real surprise to leaders to learn there were significant issues due to the lack of training practice and real case studies in the curriculum and training plan. This data was not included in the leaders' updates, and nobody else considered its importance. Useful data is the basis of root cause analysis and leads to mitigating actions.

Low engagement with frontline employees

The focus of executives is on the future, setting the direction of the organisation or the change programme. They must connect with the workforce and those making the strategy happen day to day. I work with great leaders who are genuinely interested in knowing the change team and the subject matter experts involved in the programme. The galvanising effect of this interest is evident; it makes people feel valued and connects their work with the ultimate goal. It raises motivation in a way that otherwise wouldn't happen.

Low engagement can occur in any situation, and the true intention is important, but it needs to be considered within its context. I remember visiting a call centre; the manager had a large 'open door policy' sign at the door. The intention was good, but the signal from the all-glass walls was that no comment or grievance would remain confidential for long.

Echo chamber effect

We like people who are like us and information that confirms our views. It's human nature, but it's dangerous in a leadership team; people with similar backgrounds and views reinforce each other's opinions and shut out any dissenting voices. In extreme cases, they prevent those voices from joining the conversation. I am an advocate of gender, race, age and all other diversity; however, the diversity of thinking is the one I am most passionate about because it's less visible and, thus, more challenging to achieve. It has a high correlation with the most visible diversities, so I advocate introducing those as a first step.

The long-term effects of the echo chamber are to exclude alternative ideas and emerging trends, and it can easily lead to the decline and collapse of the company.

EXAMPLE: Kodak – leaving the lens cap on

In a famous example, the leaders at Kodak ignored internal innovators advocating a move to digital products. Kodak engineer Steve Sasson invented the first digital camera in 1975. The first corporate response was, 'That's cute – but don't tell anyone about it.' The leadership attitude didn't shift, despite the results of extensive internal research by a senior executive that digital photography would take over in the long term. Even more remarkable is that the founder, George Eastman, twice before decided to give up a profitable business to invest in disruptive technology. He first moved from dry-plate to film and later chose colour over black and white, despite dominating that market and colour being of a lower quality.[12]

A pivot moment came in 1989 when the CEO retired, and the board had the choice of whether to keep supporting the film business or shift to digital. They chose the former.[13]

---

12 S Anthony, 'Kodak's Downfall Wasn't About Technology', *Harvard Business Review* (15 July 2016), https://hbr.org/2016/07/kodaks-downfall-wasnt-about-technology, accessed 23 May 2025

13 C Mui, 'How Kodak Failed', *Forbes* (18 January 2012), www.forbes.com/sites/chunkamui/2012/01/18/how-kodak-failed, accessed 23 May 2025

> The echo chamber in Kodak is the consistent confirmation within senior decision-makers that the core business is to be film and photographic chemical products rather than considering dissenting voices.

The ripple effect: How to undermine success

Blind spots have manifold impacts, including financial costs, employees' motivation and productivity suffering, and brand damage. Not listening to employees and missing customers' feedback can translate into losses if products and services no longer meet customers' needs. The Kodak example shows that not listening to internal innovators can lead to a loss of market share or even the company's demise.

Some leaders bemoan the lack of creativity and new ideas. They often don't realise these have to be nurtured by encouraging innovation and alternative options. Not doing so can demotivate employees with long-term effects; they either stay but stop trying or move on, taking their innovative thinking with them.

Sometimes blind spots lead to wrong outcomes, as in the following example.

EXAMPLE: Horizon Post Office – a miscarriage of justice

An important public inquiry took place in the UK in 2024, giving insights into leadership blind spots. The inquiry sought to ascertain the events of the Horizon Post Office scandal, which was considered one of the most significant miscarriages of justice in the country. At the core of the event is Horizon – an IT system by the Japanese company Fujitsu – rolled out across the Post Office from 1999 to manage financial transactions in branches across the country.

Since the beginning and for many years, the Post Office noticed accounting discrepancies and blamed the sub-postmasters (the people managing the branches). It has prosecuted them for theft, fraud and false accounting. The sub-postmasters denied these accusations and claimed the Horizon system was faulty. About 700 sub-postmasters were prosecuted between 2000 and 2014, suffering imprisonment, significant financial losses and damage to their reputation. It took several years for the truth to emerge and confirm that a software bug caused those financial discrepancies.

During the public inquiry, the Post Office leadership was heavily criticised for its aggressive prosecution of innocent people, failure to acknowledge the flaws in the system and lack of corporate governance.[14]

---

14 Dr R Baker and K West, 'The Post Office Scandal: A failure of governance', *IoD Policy Paper* (October 2024), www.iod.com/app/uploads/2024/10/IoD-The-Post-Office-Scandal-%E2%80%93-A-Failure-of-Governance-1-f04f78664e5242c6bebb0a01035806c2.pdf, accessed 2 April 2025

Because of the nature of blind spots, it takes time to realise there is a problem. If there is no flow of reliable information from the front line, it may be months or even longer before leaders see real and useful data on the company's state.

EXAMPLE: Marks & Spencer – not moving with the times

M&S, a stalwart of the British high street, offers another example of a leadership blind spot. From the 2000s, clothing sales started declining because the company failed to spot a change in customer preferences.[15] The company didn't realise that its core customer base of older women wanted modern clothes, and, of course, they could not attract the younger, fashionable customer segment. The leadership mistake was to pursue the same old strategy, relying on their reputation, and they misread changing customer demands. They either didn't listen to what customers were saying – if feedback from the shop floor was reaching decision-makers – or they ignored this, thinking they knew best.

This situation lasted for many years, and when it consistently hit the bottom line, the blindfold was off. Attempts to redress the poor performance then started, but it's much harder to recover from a situation that has been festering for a long time. It has only been in the past couple of years that the tide seems to have started changing.[16]

---

15   J Finch, 'Leaked Papers Reveal the Devastating Decline of M&S', *The Guardian* (7 April 2001), http://theguardian.com/business/2001/apr/07/7, accessed 2 April 2025

16   H Boland, 'M&S Loses "Grandma Shop" Image as Young Flock to Department Store', *The Telegraph* (25 December 2024), www.telegraph.co.uk/business/2024/12/25/ms-loses-grandma-shop-image-as-young-flock-to-department, accessed 2 April 2025

How to identify and avoid blind spots

It can feel a bit gloomy to consider we may have a blind spot, but there is no need. We are not failing per se; blind spots are natural human traits and we are in good company. It doesn't mean we should accept them. Instead, they are an opportunity to self-improve and to propel us – and our companies – to success.

The following illustration, adapted from the Johari window,[17] represents reducing our blind spots by getting other people to share their knowledge and insights so that – as leaders – we can make better decisions. The same applies for sharing your knowledge with others so more of it becomes public.

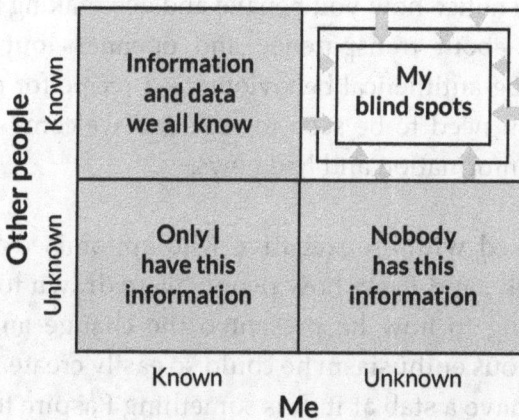

Where are the blind spots?

17 J Luft and H Ingham, *The Johari Window, A Graphic Model of Interpersonal Awareness: Proceedings of the Western Training Laboratory in Group Development* (University of California, Los Angeles, 1955)

Hold up a mirror

Anyone who believes they don't have any blind spots probably has several of them. That's why they are 'blind'. If this may be you, question yourself, your peers and your team. Coaching is beneficial, as is getting out of the office for a few days: a facilitated workshop with your top team will shake up any blind spots and long-held assumptions. Becoming self-aware of blind spots can't be solved during a half hour squeezed into a busy schedule; it's a journey of self-awareness and ongoing review.

Banish filtering by walking the talk

People notice how you behave and act: making statements about transparency and openness but then showing antithetical behaviours is a recipe for disaster. You need to be seen to seek and welcome unfiltered information and bad news.

I worked with an executive who epitomised 'walk the talk', and I saw how people were drawn to him, listening to how he presented the change and the infectious enthusiasm he could so easily create. Most of us have a stab at it. It is something I aspire to, but I am also aware that I sometimes get caught up in my bubble.

Balance agility and decisiveness

Change requires quick adjustments. Leaders are expected to be both agile and decisive, which are at the opposite ends of the spectrum. Being too agile can lead to frequent changes and no clear direction, resulting in confusion among employees and project delays. Being too decisive can lead to loss of flexibility and even the pursuit of a strategy or project that is no longer valid.

There is no easy rule on which is preferable, it depends on the situation, culture of the organisation and precedents.

Encourage alternative perspectives

This applies to team interactions (I cover group dynamics in Chapter 4). It may seem obvious, but a leader should be the last one to speak. The most effective chairpersons are silent throughout the meeting, not expressing their views even if they have a strong opinion.

Another option is assigning people to specific roles to draw out new perspectives. An external facilitator helps to burst blind spots and the echo chamber of groups.

Flip attitude to failure

Worried people don't tend to do well in any organisation. They don't innovate and – in the worst cases – hide any malpractice. A leader role modelling behaviours that support creativity and are accepting of failure creates an environment where people can flourish. People develop better product ideas when they believe there are no personal consequences if the product doesn't meet expectations.

Have a system in place to encourage failure to happen as early as possible to minimise investment costs.

Bring stories into data

Combine quantitative and qualitative information to bring data to life and have a holistic view of what customers and employees say. Numbers without a context are useless; it's a bit like assessing your investment portfolio by looking at the daily rather than long-term trends. The capability to analyse data on a profound level is essential, as it means people can extract meaning and inferences from the reams of data collected throughout the company. If data analysis skills are missing in the organisation, this is a gap that needs closing urgently.

Have reality checks with employees

I worked with a senior exec who found it difficult to go out and about and talk with employees. She worked on the top floor and was rarely seen anywhere else in the building. The only town hall I saw her present in was stilted, and you could sense the tension in the room. It's challenging for introverted people to walk around the office and chat, but it's an essential part of a leader's role and employees are appreciative of it. I have seen how a quick chat easily turned an employee from a sceptic to becoming open to listening. The advice to introvert leaders is to prioritise presenting to larger audiences and delegate smaller, interactive encounters such as skip-level meetings and 'walk the floor' to direct reports.

Recruit complementary skills

Recruiting colleagues with complementary skills will contribute an alternative perspective and bring the challenges you need to validate a change or any other initiative. I remember an enlightening conversation with a CEO who told me how his cautious and data-driven CFO perfectly balanced his gut-feeling attitude and tendency to push boundaries. I had a similar experience working for a manager with a constant stream of creative ideas, which I counterbalanced with my practical implementation questions.

His initial reaction was annoyance because he craved unequivocal enthusiasm, but then he recognised that my challenges would only strengthen his ideas into a feasible proposal.

Recognising and preventing blind spots is a long-term journey, reliant on self-awareness and honing the capability to challenge ourselves.

Summary

- Blind spots arise when we let unconscious thoughts, biases and emotions influence our behaviour. We lose impartiality, make bad decisions and experience negative outcomes. Blind spots have many impacts: financial costs, lower employee motivation and reduced productivity.

- A rapid response in a crisis makes us feel in control for acting, but it can have the opposite effect. Root cause analysis and data are the only ways to assess a problem and identify the optimal solution.

- Executives can easily get caught in a bubble, disconnected from operational levels without realistic updates about customers' and frontline employees' experiences, and unaware of emerging issues and discontent.

- Conveying (overtly or covertly) a preference for positive news or information that reinforces one's beliefs means that data gets filtered to meet this preference. Leaders are isolated from problems and resistance happening across the organisation. In the long term, this becomes an echo chamber, increasing isolation.

- Data is essential to accurate decision-making; however, to be useful, it must be accurate and relevant. Trusting data that doesn't meet these parameters is a blind spot. A blend of quantitative and qualitative data brings to life the context, captures the human side and gives a more realistic view.

- Holding up a mirror if we believe we may be immune to blind spots is the first step towards self-awareness.

- Most solutions start with changing our attitude: role modelling a culture of transparency and openness that encourages people to share unfiltered information, as well as an attitude supporting innovation, even if there is the occasional failure.

- Diversity of thinking is important, so recruit complementary skills to ensure alternative perspectives and seek the opinion of employees at all levels of the organisation. They will have useful insights and opinions.

PART TWO

FROM RESISTANCE TO COMMITMENT: UNLOCKING THE PEOPLE POTENTIAL

PART TWO

FROM RESISTANCE
TO COMMITMENT:
UNLOCKING THE PEOPLE
POTENTIAL

THREE
Pushback: Recognising And Managing Resistance

Expecting a transformation to take the shortest path through a maze is wishful thinking. I have not yet seen a project that didn't have some kind of resistance – it can take place at any level. Sometimes it's a leader not wanting his department to be reduced in numbers and importance, but more often it's employees who are worried about role changes or losing their jobs. Other times, we may not have considered what may happen. As a senior technology leader told me, 'The best plan on paper means nothing until it meets reality.'

Our role as change leaders is to make the journey as smooth as possible. This chapter is about understanding why change is hard and the cost of underestimating resistance. Ideally, we would spot signs of resistance early, making it quicker and cheaper to mitigate them. Even better is taking a long perspective: building resilience and competencies to make future changes more effortless. Effective change management isn't about eliminating resistance. By engaging rather than dismissing it, you can turn resistance into a valuable source of insight and feedback, contributing to create a change journey that is inclusive, thoughtful and, ultimately, more successful.

My experience: Learning what change is all about

My first project got me hooked on change management. I was told the project objective was straightforward: transitioning a team of back-office employees into front-office roles, handling customer queries and delivering an exceptional customer experience. I had never done anything like this, so I had no expectations and I believed it when I was told it would be easy. I soon discovered this was a seismic change for the people involved.

It wasn't just any team; it was a group of ex-phone engineers in Scotland, a cohort of technical experts who had spent years – decades, in some cases – working in the field. Their job had been self-sufficient, technical and straightforward: drive long distances to telephone exchanges and customer homes, solve technical problems and then move on to the next task. Their customer interactions were brief and factual, driven by efficiency rather than building rapport. Even their current back-office role didn't require any customer interaction. They were being asked to perform a polar opposite role: engaging directly with customers, defusing tensions and creating positive experiences. For them, the change felt deeply unsettling.

Once I got to the office on my first day, I knew this wouldn't be easy. The team made it clear that they didn't want their role to change. Here I was, a young woman from headquarters parachuted in to tell them how to do their jobs differently. It was clear from the onset that they saw me as an outsider, someone who didn't understand what it was like to be in their shoes.

I started by getting them to understand the importance of customer experience. They considered customers to be obstacles – people they needed to deal with briefly before moving on to their next task. The concept of creating an exceptional customer experience seemed unnecessary, even frivolous. Why bother when you might never see that customer again?

To make the concept more tangible, I immersed them in customer journeys. I covered the office walls with all the customer touchpoints, describing a real scenario from the first call to the resolution of the issue. I also initiated group discussions, hoping to spark interest in the customer's perspective. My efforts fell flat. I could see the boredom in their eyes, the resistance bubbling just below the surface. I needed something that would resonate personally.

I flipped the script, and instead of talking about abstract customer experiences, I asked them to think of a recent purchase that had gone wrong. One mentioned a botched fridge delivery, and we began mapping out his customer journey. It was a breakthrough moment. As we walked through his experience – frustration, delays, poor communication – the team began to connect the dots. They started to see what it was like to be on the other side, in the customer's shoes.

This exercise was a turning point, but it was just the beginning. While I had made some progress in getting them to think differently about their roles, I knew I hadn't yet won them over. I was tolerated, not accepted.

This perception manifested itself in small but telling ways. For example, I scheduled morning meetings only to find myself alone in the meeting room. I later learnt that my chosen time (free in their diaries) clashed with their routine tea break in the canteen – a ritual nobody had thought to mention, let alone invite me to.

Recognising my mistake, I adapted. I set up early morning 'come for a free breakfast' Friday sessions before the day's official start. It was a game-changer. Free food was an effective incentive and people started showing up. These informal get-togethers were invaluable for building rapport and talking about concerns in a relaxed setting. They also helped me introduce the idea that they couldn't all take breaks simultaneously during working hours – a subtle but essential shift towards understanding the demands of their new roles.

The project stretched for several months and wasn't without its challenges. Beyond the behavioural shifts I was trying to instil, they had to attend training on newly introduced processes and systems. Resistance continued to rear its head, as it often does. A step forward seemed to be met with a step back as the ex-engineers clung to their old habits.

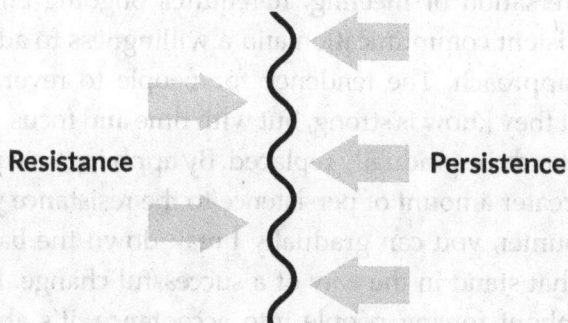

Resistance   **Persistence**

The persistence to resistance ratio

Months later, after the project finished and I happened to be back in that office, one of the engineers, who had been the most resistant, pulled me aside. 'Thank you,' he said. 'I'd lost my enthusiasm for the job, but this new role has given me a new purpose.' It was a significant victory. I learnt that change, though difficult, can lead to renewed energy and satisfaction in one's job.

This project was a lesson in the reality of managing resistance to change, that addressing the human side is more important than any new processes or systems. It's about understanding people's fears, giving them space to make sense of the change and guiding them – sometimes gently, sometimes firmly – towards a new way of thinking and working.

I learnt that persistence is essential to manage resistance because the latter never disappears after a single conversation or meeting. It requires ongoing effort, consistent communication and a willingness to adapt the approach. The tendency for people to revert to what they know is strong, but with time and focus, old habits can be gradually replaced. By applying an equal or greater amount of persistence to the resistance you encounter, you can gradually break down the barriers that stand in the way of a successful change. It is not about forcing people into acceptance, it's about understanding their reactions, addressing their fears and concerns, and guiding them through the process with empathy and support. It is not about ticking off change activities but recognising it's an emotional journey. The better you understand and manage the emotional aspects of change, the more likely you are to achieve the desired benefits and ROI.

Why change feels so hard: The role of emotions

Experiencing resistance to change sparked my desire to find new ways to overcome it. Even when the change is beneficial, people often push back, sometimes subtly and other times quite openly. The reasons behind this resistance are rarely rooted in rational thought; instead, they stem from an emotional reaction.

That's why trying to convince someone to embrace change by presenting rational arguments – less admin, greater efficiency, more opportunities – hits a brick wall. These logical reasons don't address the true sources. Mitigating resistance requires digging deeper to uncover what's driving those emotional reactions.

Fear of the unknown

The fear of the unknown is a reason for resisting change. We handle uncertainty differently. Some people thrive on the thrill of the unknown, always seeking out new challenges. For others, the unknown is something to be avoided at all costs. For them, change represents a leap into uncharted territory, which can be terrifying.

As change leaders, we need to recognise and manage these different attitudes towards uncertainty. Understanding these differences will help tailor the change approach to meet people where they are, providing the right support to help them navigate the unknown.

Loss of control

Loss of control can be experienced by anybody, including those in positions of influence. Change can feel like a runaway train – once it starts moving, it can be hard to steer it, let alone stop. For a business leader, this loss of control can be deeply unsettling. They may worry about losing their hold on all they have achieved so far. This fear isn't limited to those at the top. Employees with their career path mapped out may suddenly feel threatened by a reorganisation, fearing the change will derail their plans.

This fear can manifest in subtle ways, such as a department head obstructing discussions or delaying decisions. On the surface, their objections might seem logical – for example, 'we can't train everyone on multiple sites in time' – but digging deeper can uncover the underlying fear of losing control. These individuals may not even be fully aware of their fear, so open conversations are useful for uncovering it.

Threat to competence

A change programme invariably means changing how people work, which can involve improving or learning new skills, for example, specialised digital skills or the capability to work with emerging technologies. Some employees experience resistance towards having to learn new skills, and may resent it if it is presented as the only way to keep their job. They may fear being unable to learn new skills (especially if they have not done so for a long time) and resentful that their previous experience doesn't seem to count. Underlying these emotions is a threat to their job security. It is more common among people who have been in the same company – often the same job – for a long time.

Fear of failure

Change may require people to step out of their comfort zones, take on new responsibilities or learn new skills. They may fear being unable to meet expectations, leading to resistance. This fear is more prevalent in high-stakes environments where the consequences of failure are perceived to be significant. Fear of failure can be particularly acute among business leaders, who may fear a loss of credibility, influence or even their jobs if they cannot successfully manage the change.

These fears make change hard. There is comfort in the status quo, the stability of your team and the work you know well.

The high price of mismanaging resistance

When assessing projects in their later stages or post go-live – when an expensive new system was supposed to integrate functions, optimise operations and make them super-efficient, but it didn't achieve any savings or extra revenue – I talk with executives unsure of where things went wrong. The assessment usually shows the root cause is often related to people. It is not the employees' fault in the sense that they are not sabotaging the change on purpose. The reality is that employees need to be taken on a journey, not just told, 'Here is the new system/process/organisational structure, let's get on with it.' That's why giving a vision of the change, showing what it means for them and facilitating the journey are essential.

The assessment sometimes uncovers more bad news: the cost is felt in the long term. Addressing the issue post-implementation will add time and costs, and a demotivated workforce will become less productive over time, thus denting profitability even more. This often leads to less trust in the leadership team, creating a negative loop.

It doesn't have to be like this. Project failure is a possibility, but it's not inevitable. What's needed is the inclusion of a change strategy that considers the employee experience and behavioural shifts and is integral to any transformation programme. It doesn't even mean you need a full-time change team; what you need is expertise. It saves you money.

My experience: Employee engagement as a lever of change success

In this outsourcing, I achieved high employee engagement and paved the way for a successful transformation in the future. The client was adamant about wanting a positive employee experience, avoiding bad press and repercussions on their well-regarded brand. As a change manager, this was an excellent opportunity to develop an optimal experience centred on the employee and to deliver the most benefits for the company.

The approach was based on high engagement and several interactions for employees to learn about the change and, most importantly, to ask questions and talk with executives and the project team. There was a clear journey with key events and dates so that employees could see the next steps. They knew when a decision was expected of them and were supported by executives and the project team to make those decisions. There was a clear vision for the future and a great image representing the journey that soon became a highly recognisable symbol of the programme. The executive team was pivotal to success; they were highly involved in town halls and other presentations across the impacted locations.

I consistently measured employee engagement, motivation and perceptions of the change throughout the programme. The baseline was the regular employee engagement survey to give me a before-we-even-started view. Right after the change was announced, I took the first direct measure: a sample survey of employees from both the impacted teams and others, which gave a useful reference point. I facilitated focus groups to gather more qualitative data and personal experiences and performed sentiment analysis. In addition, there was a comprehensive change impact assessment (CIA), which gave me mitigation actions to keep the team busy for many months. Progress tracking was essential for both change interventions and employee engagement, to have useful insights on what was working and what was not, and make the necessary adjustments.

This complex programme was a success. The number of employees choosing to move exceeded expectations, which benefited both companies. There were some challenging moments, delays and other issues along the way. The focus on employees and openness created the trust needed to deal with the blips. Employee engagement and productivity measures remained high throughout, leading to successful outcomes.

Resistance signals you may be missing

Some executives are often surprised when they come across resistance at the midpoint or later in the implementation. Most of the time, the signs have been there but haven't been spotted. How do you recognise the signs of resistance early?

The increase in hybrid and remote working adds to the complexity of this question, since managers don't see and may not talk with their team members as frequently. Given that this is a more challenging scenario, I will prioritise how to notice resistance among remote workers.

These are the most frequent signs of resistance:

- **Rise in absenteeism.** There is HR data on absences; however, people working from home fall easily under the radar, as they may be unofficially absent. There are several tools to track whether employees are actively online, but

I am reluctant to rely on those as they can erode trust. It is often only over the medium term that it becomes apparent if someone has not been performing and meeting their objectives. In the short term, the line manager is more likely to notice rising levels of absenteeism.

- **Low engagement in meetings.** Similar to absenteeism, this is harder to notice for remote workers. Apart from non-attendance, other signs are low interaction or people with the camera off during calls. Having worked in several companies where most meetings were online, I find the culture around camera use very telling, if only circumstantial evidence, of low engagement. This is a situation when it's important for leaders to role model engagement behaviours. I have asked senior or influential employees to be on camera to encourage this behaviour and create pressure among others to be seen.

- **Gossip and rumours.** I have often learnt more about employees' experience of a change by hanging around the office kitchen area than from the most sophisticated surveys. Listening to how employees describe the change and the language they use are good indicators of whether they understand the purpose and outcomes of the change. As an external consultant and impartial listener, conversations I overhear are kept confidential; however, they represent valuable insights and help me tweak a project.

- **Quiet quitting.** Some form of micro resistance has always been present; employees go through the motions and do the minimum they can get away with, with no real engagement with the change programme. The term 'quiet quitting' gained widespread attention in the past couple of years – one of the post-pandemic shifts in the workplace. There are several factors behind quiet quitting and therefore any solution is rooted in its causes, which can vary from prioritising work-life balance to burnout, not seeing any career prospects and more. It's important to remember that it's a waste for both the individual and the business.

Change leaders need to be on the lookout for signs of resistance and identify the root causes (as different causes call for different interventions) – not forgetting prevention: shaping a change strategy that minimises the potential for resistance.

There's a final, fairly controversial point: in some situations, I advocate active rather than passive resistance. As we see from the change curve below, denial is a sticky place; some people may be stuck there for a long time and unable to let go of the past. The premise of active resistance is that any issues can only be addressed once they come to the surface.

As an example from many years ago, when I was working in a consulting company and still a little naive, I was in a meeting with a prospective client as part of the bid negotiations. I was asked how I would manage employees who were in denial about a major change involving a restructuring and who were not engaging with communications. My answer, 'Make them angry,' was probably too direct. I would not reply like this today; however, I still believe it's important to create a space where people can vent their emotions as part of their journey to acceptance. We won the bid, so maybe it was not a bad answer after all.

The change curve is an essential tool for leaders too

The Kübler-Ross Change Curve[18] is one of the most effective tools for understanding and managing people's emotional responses to change. It was developed to describe the stages of grief; however, the curve is equally applicable to the emotions people experience during organisational change. The stages are not necessarily linear, and people can move back and forth between them. The five stages are:

1. **Denial.** Employees and leaders convince themselves that the change is unnecessary,

---

18   E Kübler-Ross, *On Death and Dying: What the dying have to teach doctors, nurses, clergy & their own families* (Scribner Book Company, 2014)

irrelevant or unlikely to affect them. Common phrases include: 'This is just a passing trend' or 'We've always done it this way, and it works fine.'

2. **Anger.** Frustration sets in as the reality of the change begins to hit. Blame is directed towards leadership, consultants or external circumstances. The chatter includes: 'This is going to ruin everything!' or 'Why didn't anyone ask us?'

3. **Depression.** Morale hits rock bottom as the challenges of implementation become apparent. Employees lose motivation, and leaders second-guess the decision. Expect sighs of despair like: 'We've wasted so much money,' or 'Maybe we should just scrap the whole thing.'

4. **Bargaining.** Stakeholders try to negotiate their way out of full-scale change, proposing compromises that dilute the effort. Typical comments might be: 'What if we only implement the easy parts?' or 'Can't we keep the old system running alongside the new one?'

5. **Acceptance.** The organisation begins to adapt, finding new ways to operate effectively. Teams collaborate, momentum builds and leaders start celebrating small wins. The sentiment shifts to: 'We've come this far – let's see it through.'

The pace of progressing through the change curve is also variable; some people may whizz through it, while others may be stuck in one stage forever. It is a useful tool for assessing where individuals and teams are emotionally in the change process.

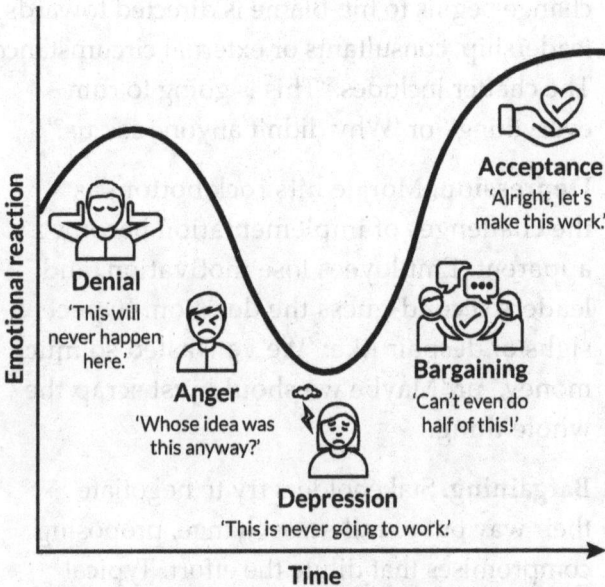

The change curve

I use the change curve in conversations with leaders to set expectations of likely employees' reactions. It can highlight a blind spot I have seen many times and is illustrated by the change curve itself. Leaders start on the journey early; they discuss the need for a change (a new strategy, operating model or system), put the foundations in place and start engaging with any external parties. This can take several months, and by the time the change initiative is announced, they are likely to have been in the acceptance phase for a while.

When leaders present the change and sense resistance, they forget two essential conditions:

1. **They initiated and controlled the change, therefore they will always be in a position of greater choice and control.** As we have seen, loss of control is a primary reason why change is hard. This applies even if the change was triggered by an external factor, i.e. loss of market share or threat of acquisition. They may have experienced denial and anger but they took control.

2. **Employees have not yet gone through the curve and must be allowed the time and space to do so.** I see leaders forget their journey and how unsettling the beginnings were. Rather than apportion blame on people and prod them along with rational arguments, it is better to have a structure in place with actions to facilitate the journey.

The change curve truly comes to life in one to ones and workshops with employees. They find it a useful tool as a basis for talking about the change; it normalises the emotional turmoil they may feel and helps them relate to the situation. This conversation requires underlying trust.

Sometimes, I share my personal experiences of being on the curve. For example, some years ago, I had a health scare and I vividly remember my journey of moving – with great difficulty – along the curve. Even knowing about the theory couldn't stop it from happening. It applies to any situation when a change is 'imposed'; I remember feeling the loss of control and, most vividly, being in denial.

Building bridges: Solutions for overcoming resistance

Senior executives may not directly deal with employee resistance, but it's their responsibility to ensure the programme and management teams actively manage it. The following options both prevent and manage resistance.

Align incentives to encourage acceptance and adoption

The ideal solution or new state should be as easy and appealing as possible. If the new system is intuitive to use and saves time and effort, you are on to a winner. In this case, people need to know about it as early as possible and preferably practise with the new technology. Arranging a demonstration is the most useful means for people to familiarise themselves with a new system.

Associate the change purpose to something people value. This can range from personal (i.e. development opportunities) to societal purposes (i.e. environmental protection and B-corp status).

Rewards can be used to encourage acceptance. An example of this would be linking objectives to the desired outcomes of the change, noting that rewards are not necessarily financial but any positive outcome in exchange for an action. In an enterprise resource planning system roll-out in HR, I made it explicit in both the line manager and employee objectives that they had to use the online capture form for one-to-one meeting notes and performance reviews. The implied reward was the data provided as input to end-year performance evaluation and a pay rise or bonus. The change applied equally to managers and employees, thus giving them both ownership and an incentive to ensure that the other party would comply.

Be proactive

Get some employees actively involved in the change. This will make them feel like they have a stake in its success. I noticed the positive impact this made in my early projects and used it ever since.

The more effective results tend to happen once employees start discussing how to improve a process, give suggestions and volunteer to be involved. Once an employee has done all this work and their suggestion has been approved, they feel ownership and won't let it fail. The same principle applies to senior stakeholders, with the sponsor primarily responsible for involving their senior peers so they have a stake in the project.

Equip and support managers. There are two important aspects:

- The change impacts managers directly. Issues arise in HR projects when people managers see the change as an added burden on their already heavy workload. If the change means more work in the short term, be open, recognise the more significant initial effort and set the expectation of a long-term improvement, then link the additional effort to a reward.

- The assumption that managers can easily face the brunt of employee resistance. It is an unfair expectation; some managers are excellent in their aptitude to manage change, while for others, it is a struggle. Essentially, one can't become a skilled psychologist on demand. Managers need to be equipped with skills to recognise and manage resistance. Supporting them and giving them the right skills will allow them to help their team through the journey. Tools such as communication templates and FAQs are helpful but they may not be enough. More effective are learning and courses, especially role play to develop long-term useful skills.

Communicate what's most important. I will cover communications in Chapter 6, but I can't miss a brief mention here. Effective communications are about answering the key questions: 'Why?' and 'What's in it for me?' The answers need to be about the audience. Always consider what is first and foremost crucial to employees.

Get influencers on board. I used to call them early adopters or natural leaders (those people who, no matter the job title, seem to get others revolving around and listening to them), but this is about influencing your co-workers, not just being an early user. Many change managers like to set up a network of change agents; it's suitable in some cases, but often it does not warrant the effort to create and manage one. I like the informality and the innovative spirit of having natural leaders who already know how to lead and early adopters who are naturally enthusiastic about a new system or strategy.

More options to check resistance among remote workers

Tools based on the experience sampling method. These are customarily used to capture real-time emotional state data, mostly in research on happiness and to measure the impact of daily activities on well-being. They can be used in change programmes with a sample of employees, who receive prompts via a mobile app or text asking how they are feeling about the change and to rate their emotional state on a scale. They are useful because they're timely and quick.

Make calls interactive with poll questions. This is especially effective in large calls, interspersing serious and fun questions. The poll can check people are still there and awake! Because you get immediate responses, they are useful for obtaining immediate reactions from attendees as well as fairly truthful responses, since they are anonymous. Only reveal the final responses when the poll is closed to avoid bias and groupthink.

My experience: Making time for others to facilitate change

A project I led some years ago involved moving employees from one company to another. It was complex from an HR and legal perspective, with changes to terms and conditions, pension, insurance and so on. Impacted employees were based in offices across multiple cities and I used to travel to them for meetings and to share updates. I always included time with the employees affected, who were still making sense of the change and deciding whether to accept the offer to move company or lose their jobs. It was a tough choice as many had worked there for a long time. I used to chat with individuals over a cup of coffee (or tea after I had too many coffees that day). The important point is that I could not answer any critical questions about pensions and benefits (we had a dedicated team of legal and financial advisers). Still, I knew (and was later told) how vital these informal chats were for them. Knowing that someone from the programme team cared enough to talk with them helped shift many of them from resistance to acceptance. This is one of the most essential tools for a change leader: the power of caring and making time for others.

Summary

- There will always be some resistance: identify where in the organisation it is most likely to emerge and the root causes. By identifying resistance early, it will be quicker and cheaper to mitigate it.

- The role of change leaders is to make the journey as smooth as possible and, ideally, to build resilience so that future changes become easier. Leaders and other influential stakeholders are role models and must be visible change supporters.

- Change isn't about implementing new processes or systems. It's about addressing the human side of transformation: understanding people's fears and giving them time and space to make sense of the change. Create a vision and map a journey showing what it means for them and clarifying what you expect of them.

- Resistance is rooted in emotional reactions – fear of the unknown, loss of control, threat to competence and fear of failure – and can't be overcome with rational arguments. The more resistance some leaders see and the more they use logical arguments, the more this loop has to be broken.

- Be attuned to signs of resistance – absenteeism, low engagement in meetings, gossip and rumours, and quiet quitting – especially among remote workers.

- Measure employee engagement, motivation, and perceptions of the change consistently throughout the programme to identify pockets of resistance and quickly define targeted change interventions.

- Solutions to prevent and manage resistance include aligning incentives to encourage acceptance and adoption.

- Change management isn't about eliminating resistance; it's about engaging with people as a valuable source of insight and feedback. Persistence is essential to managing resistance because it never disappears after a single conversation or meeting. It requires ongoing effort, consistent communication and a willingness to adapt the approach.

FOUR

Inside The Mind: The Role Of Behavioural Insights

People don't change through the sheer force of logical arguments; successful change relies on understanding and managing emotional reactions. No logical argument can solve people's behaviour when it is driven by emotional and psychological factors. This clash is a lose-lose situation. Since we can't overhaul human psychology, the only solution is to step away from logical arguments and the rational approach.

This chapter examines three elements that are essential to understanding human behaviours during change:

1. Psychological safety

2. Cognitive biases

3. Cognitive overload

The solutions to creating success and a better change experience are based on leveraging social influences and creating new habits. They are valuable in any situation, from influencing shareholders, to dealing with group dynamics to getting people to support organisational change.

The role of psychological safety in building trust

Safety is one of the most important human needs. In the context of organisational change, the emphasis is on psychological safety. Change can trigger fear, uncertainty and an unsettled working environment. None of these are conducive to employees' motivation and support for change. Creating psychological safety gives people the space to make sense of the change and facilitates their journey along the change curve (see Chapter 3).

Psychological safety is defined as a shared belief that a team is a safe place where people can share ideas, ask questions and make (and admit to) mistakes without fear of retribution or humiliation. This concept is at the core of Amy Edmondson's research.[19] A professor of leadership and management at Harvard Business School, she seeks to understand how individuals and organisations can foster such work environments.

19   A Edmondson, *The Fearless Organization: Creating psychological safety in the workplace for learning, innovation, and growth* (Wiley, 2018)

Change projects involve something new, from technological innovation to changing how people work and interact. Some projects are about creating a culture of creativity and innovation. The underlying need is, therefore, to collaborate, test ideas and communicate openly. Human beings have a switch that stops us from trusting others if we sense danger (we would not have made it out of the caves and would have fallen prey to wild animals otherwise). It's not as dramatic, but something similar happens at work. If we don't feel safe, we withhold ideas and comments, avoid taking risks and remain silent if we see a potential issue. It is a cost for the organisation. We may also hide problems. One transformation leader I spoke with told me about a time in his company when a post-acquisition issue was minimised because an employee escalated it immediately. This is the way he described the corporate culture he created, 'It's not a problem to have a problem; it's a problem to hide it.'

One of Edmondson's early studies involved observing medical teams and their ability to learn from mistakes. She discovered that teams who reported higher rates of error had better performance outcomes. It may seem counter-intuitive, but it shows that if people feel safe to ask for help, discuss mistakes and ask for feedback, the outcome is growth and performance improvements for the whole team. The medical profession is an excellent example because it's a dynamic and pressurised environment with access to rich data, where decisions truly mean life or death. The lessons apply to the business environment as well.

What can you do as a leader to foster psychological safety?

First, role model the behaviours that are the foundations of psychological safety, such as admitting to mistakes (and what you have learnt from them) and asking for feedback. This may be onerous and counterproductive for a C-suite officer; the advice is to be selective and choose examples that best show (smaller) mistakes and focus on the growth experience. Adjusting the journey of change is to be expected, as one leader told me: 'Corrective measures are not a weakness – they are how change works in reality.'

Second, reward desirable behaviours. For example, suppose the business aims to develop new products and features. In that case, employees need to be rewarded for their effort and creativity, not punished for the wrong feature or a product not meeting its specifications. The latter gives the wrong signals; next time, people won't even try. The advice is to introduce checkpoints earlier in the process to stop products or projects before too much effort and cost are invested. It may even be worth rewarding people who stop projects and products in the early stages!

Finally, encourage challenging conversations. Feedback requires time, effort and a lot of practice, and it is often done poorly in many companies. Improving this would be a small thing with a significant positive impact. Many managers and employees still find it awkward to give and receive feedback. One cause is the inability to deal with difficult situations and to explain the need to correct something in a manner that encourages an individual's growth, rather than making them feel demotivated. I advise agreeing in advance on what shape the feedback should take and encouraging people to proactively seek feedback, instead of being on the receiving end. By reframing feedback and linking it to personal growth, we will have a useful tool for both managers and their teams.

Cognitive biases: The brain's shortcuts that derail change

People instinctively will reject a change imposed on them, so we must take an alternative perspective and understand their fears, anxieties and expectations.

In Chapter 3, we covered fear of the unknown and loss of control. Here, we delve into more complex biases to better understand people's responses and design the most appropriate mitigating actions. Uncovering and managing biases is not straightforward. The suggested mitigations are the starting point and require adapting to the specific context of employees and organisations.

Status quo

This is the preference for keeping things as they are, simply because they are familiar and have served us well in the past. This can apply to anybody, from the CEO who is reluctant to critically examine the strategy that he defined years ago but is no longer profitable, to the sales assistant who doesn't want to be on the shop floor helping customers and prefers the comfort of standing behind the counter.

Mitigations include positioning the change as an opportunity rather than a threat ('what's in it for me?') or demonstrating the tangible and intangible costs of maintaining the status quo. We can also reduce resistance by encouraging people to start with small, incremental changes and build on each new adjustment.

Loss aversion

We fear losses more than we value equivalent gains. We worry about what we may lose from the change, even when it's clear that the benefits outweigh the risks. This may cause leaders to avoid making necessary decisions or employees to not realise they may learn useful skills because of a change of role.

It may seem unlikely, but it's possible to reframe the change as a gain, focusing on the benefits and opportunities. Make sure employees can relate to the gains. Another reframing option is to show the risks of not changing; in this case, position inaction as a loss. Underlying these options, it's important to offer reassurance to manage any underlying fears that people may have.

Confirmation bias

We seek out information that proves our beliefs and decisions and ignore anything that contradicts them. The problem is when change leaders stick to their preferred course of action and ignore any new information, risks or dissenting voices. Or employees may interpret data through the lens of fear, thus reinforcing their resistance to change.

A mitigation for leaders is to encourage alternative perspectives from the start of the project so this approach becomes the norm. For employees, it is important to have early visibility into what is new (be it a system or new job description) so that they can start experimenting and making sense of the change.

Anchoring bias

We use the first piece of information we come across as an anchor, which makes people inflexible when new data emerges that requires a shift. I have seen this happen in technology programs lasting several years. New information is likely to emerge during this time; however, if we anchor our understanding on an early fact about the change, it is hard to modify our expectations. This is a particular issue since the information available at the start is often minimal.

A mitigation for leaders is to include regular checkpoints in the plan to challenge the project and its progress. This will shift behaviours towards acceptance that things may change as well as reducing the hold of the anchor. Moreover, change leads need to position the shift carefully at the beginning or even hold onto communications until there is more accurate information.

Optimism bias

Optimism is a good thing, isn't it? Not if it causes leaders to overestimate the likelihood of the positive and underestimate the negatives. The effects are unrealistic timelines, insufficient resources and poor risk planning. There may be too much optimism at the beginning of a project when the change impacts are not well defined and people have not considered all the implications, so they are more open to change. As we reach the launch and the impacts become real, resistance emerges.

A mitigation for leaders is to include both positive and negative inputs in every leadership conversation about the change so people are forced to consider both. Employees should be encouraged to engage and ask questions. The sooner they get involved, the quicker they are to accept.

Cognitive overload: When constant change takes its toll

Individually or jointly, overload and fatigue impact how people experience a change. Cognitive overload happens when the quantity of information a person is asked to process and retain exceeds their capacity (in cognitive psychology, it refers explicitly to the working memory used). When that happens, the individual can find it harder to learn, engage, problem-solve and make decisions. I am sure we can all relate to this feeling.

During a period of change, employees are asked to deal with uncertainty, learn new systems and processes, and work with new colleagues or within a new team structure. There is always a wider context; we all have things happening in our personal lives. The overload and emotional turmoil caused by the change can lead to confusion and loss of productivity, as well as mistakes impacting long-term performance.

Change fatigue is the mental and emotional exhaustion people experience when subjected to frequent or continuous changes. It is about the cumulative effect of responding to and trying to adapt to change.

Like other types of exhaustion, think of fatigue as a glass of water. As more drops are added, the water level gets close to the rim and when no more drops can fit, the water starts to spill over.

Organisations constantly shift their strategic direction, restructuring and technology updates. Leaders seek the 'perfect' set-up and can be overenthusiastic in their pursuit, not paying enough attention to how employees may experience the situation. The latter need time to adjust and stabilise; otherwise, the effect is disengagement, low morale and a decline in productivity.

What can you do about cognitive overload?

The first question for leaders is: 'Do you really need to add more change?' It is useful for the executive team to mind map all the (main) change programmes – live and planned – and capture how they are interconnected. Sometimes, just looking at this visual is enough to draw attention to the plight of employees; other times, it becomes evident that some are in conflict. Having facilitated these mind mapping discussions and the costs, both to implement the change and from any loss of productivity from overload and fatigue, I have seen the room go really quiet.

Here are some suggestions of how to handle overload and fatigue:

- **Prioritise change.** Not all change initiatives are needed. Prioritise them based on strategic importance, and be willing to cut out projects if they don't meet the criteria. Consider which part of the organisation or employee groups will be impacted to avoid too much change for the same group.

- **Simplify communications.** The more content people receive, the less likely they are to read, let alone absorb it. Lengthy emails are often ignored. Instead, focus on three key changes and then explain five (as a maximum) things that will change.

- **Provide micro-learning.** Gone are the days of putting people in a training room for days. Break content down into smaller chunks, make them available at the point of need and use the most suitable media. Remember that true learning happens during practice.

- **Incorporate downtime.** Learning from sport, athletes understand the importance of rest and recovery time. Use the same thinking to create stabilisation periods, giving employees time to adjust before the next inevitable period of change.

Cognitive overload and change fatigue are significant barriers to organisational change. They should not be disregarded as 'people will just get on with it'.

They can cause a programme to fail to meet the planned benefits and raise costs considerably.

Harnessing the power of social influence

A less-used behavioural change intervention – albeit a powerful one – is leveraging social norms. Humans are social creatures and we tend to follow and conform to what others do, even while taking pride in our individuality. Why do we have this tendency to be followers? We seek safety and security. Our brains have developed to seek acceptance by the group as a means to ensure food and protection.

The fight–flee–freeze reaction

Here is a small but useful piece of practical advice: if you are ever unsure about how someone may react to any event, ask yourself, 'What would a cave person do in that situation?' The answer will be pretty accurate. The human brain has evolved, but the limbic system still dominates, giving us instinctive reactions and emotions. That's the system that gives us the fight–flee–freeze reaction, and it's very active in stressful situations. Since change is often stressful, it's good to know how our brains work and how to manage emotional reactions.

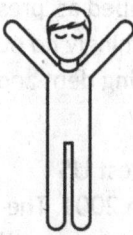

Fight	Flee	Freeze
'I am going to get it done my way'	'I am going to get out of here'	'I am not sure what to do, let's wait and see'

The fight–flee–freeze reaction

The effect of social norms

Social norms are the unwritten rules that influence behaviours in a group. They are shared expectations that develop over time and are observed in organisations and society. Social norms are important at work because they motivate individuals to behave in what is deemed the preferred and acceptable way, and thus conform to what they see others doing. It is important to consider that this works for negative as well as positive behaviours.

The effect of social norms can be observed in some high-profile cases.

EXAMPLE: Enron – the road to bankruptcy

Enron's leadership promoted a highly competitive and aggressive working environment, pressuring employees with unattainable targets, aware that not meeting those meant losing their job. A culture described as 'pressure-cooker' left some employees with seemingly no other option than to behave unethically, hiding debt and inflating profits.

Enron went from being one of the largest US corporations to filing for bankruptcy in 2001. The investigation found persistent fraudulent accounting and insider trading. The ramifications of the scandal included the prosecution of senior executives and the collapse of their accounting firm Arthur Andersen. It led to the Sarbanes-Oxley Act of 2002, aimed at improving corporate governance and financial reporting standards – not to forget losses for employee through their pension and retirement funds.[20,21]

Although we all think we would never behave that way, consider what it would feel like working in that kind of environment: the pressure from your manager (from the CEO downward) demanding more profits, knowing your colleagues are hiding the truth about debts and that there is no governance or checks in place. Most people would either leave (flee) or adapt (a kind of freeze of values and beliefs). An individual can rarely fight an organisation of that size alone, although there are brave whistleblowers who do so.

---

20 CNN Editorial Research, 'Enron Fast Facts', CNN (18 April 2025), https://edition.cnn.com/2013/07/02/us/enron-fast-facts/index.html, accessed 25 April 2025

21 J Stephens and P Behr, 'Enron's Culture Fed Its Demise', *The Washington Post* (27 January 2002), www.washingtonpost.com/archive/politics/2002/01/27/enrons-culture-fed-its-demise/d73cf80c-0d00-4281-848d-968683828ef9, accessed 25 April 2025

Examples like this make social norms relevant in the workplace. No matter the rules, we are less likely to follow them if nobody else does.

The good news is that we can use social norms positively to drive and embed change. It starts from the top; leaders can leverage social norms to create an environment where desired behaviours become the expected and accepted way of working. Here is how:

- **Set the social norms.** Identify which behaviours align with the planned change. If collaboration is an essential basis of the change, identify which existing behaviours reinforce collaboration and which new ones are needed. For example, set up team (rather than individual) targets and organise the space to increase collaboration for office-based people or online tools for remote workers. The specific behavioural interventions depend on company culture. Storytelling is a powerful means to create social norms, as it captures and shares stories of employees demonstrating the desired behaviours.

- **Leverage peer influence.** People are influenced by what others do, especially those we respect and identify with. I mentioned the role of 'influencers' in Chapter 3; in any company, there are people who are widely respected, no matter their job title. Seeing influential employees embrace the change makes it more likely for wider groups to follow. It is a process that should be guided rather than mandated. The best course of action is to observe and measure the uptake of change and intervene with tweaks if required. The ripple effect of embedding change is more sustainable if driven by a colleague.

- **Communicate in the 'norm' way.** This is a subtle yet more powerful and effective way of communicating; rather than telling people what to do, you tell them what their peers have done. For example, instead of saying, 'You must complete the customer service training,' state '80% of employees have already completed the customer service training.' The emphasis is on what colleagues have done, encouraging others to do the same and reiterating the messages to reinforce the norms over time. Suppose you want to establish a learning culture. This will need to be mentioned frequently and in different contexts, highlighting what employees have achieved by devoting more time to learning.

Leveraging social norms is more valuable and powerful because it's subtle and creates an environment that encourages change. I once used it to encourage a sales team to adopt a new CRM system. The initial uptake was low; they didn't like to enter data in a system, coming up with all sorts of excuses. I analysed the data and found a couple of examples of early adopters. My change intervention was to showcase the success of these early adopters and top performers who were using the CRM system to boost sales and their bonuses. The rest of the team quickly followed.

My experience: Keeping it simple for maximum results

I was leading a system implementation impacting thousands of people across the world. It was a significant change, and this dawned on us when we started planning comms and learning: there was so much content for people to understand and implement.

I saw the first draft of the comms and got into a conundrum: should we give people all this information, risk overload, and, consequently, people not taking notice? I decided not, and challenged the comms team to reduce the content to the most basic they could. It was not a popular request. They were used to pushing out maximum content; the mantra was 'people need to know everything.' In this case, I had to manage resistance within the project team, not just executives and employees.

It took some iterations, resulting in a great campaign with simple and concise messages delivered at the right time. For the comms team, it represented a change in perspective, emphasising timing and audiences; for example, some of the content was only needed at specific times – i.e. performance reviews or before leave requests – or only by some people. Choosing simplification and targeting was a good learning, and an approach I have taken ever since.

Breaking habits and building better ones

This has become one of my go-to change interventions. Breaking old patterns and creating new habits is central to the success of organisational change. We are getting people to move away from old patterns and form new habits and routines. How does it work?

The cue, routine, reward model

The cue, routine, reward model (introduced by Charles Duhigg in *The Power of Habit*)[22] describes how habits are created and embedded. Habits develop when a specific trigger (cue) prompts employees to undertake an activity or behaviour (routine), which is reinforced by a positive outcome (reward).

The cue can be either an internal state (i.e. the time of day, location or emotional state) or an external event. The routine is the automatic behaviour that follows, such as checking the phone or reaching for a snack. The reward is a positive outcome – a sense of satisfaction or relief that reinforces the routine. The brain remembers this loop, which strengthens with every repetition.

22   C Duhigg, *The Power of Habit: Why we do what we do, and how to change* (Cornerstone Digital, 2012)

Routine
The autopilot
takes over

Cue
The spark
that starts
it all

Reward
The taste
of success

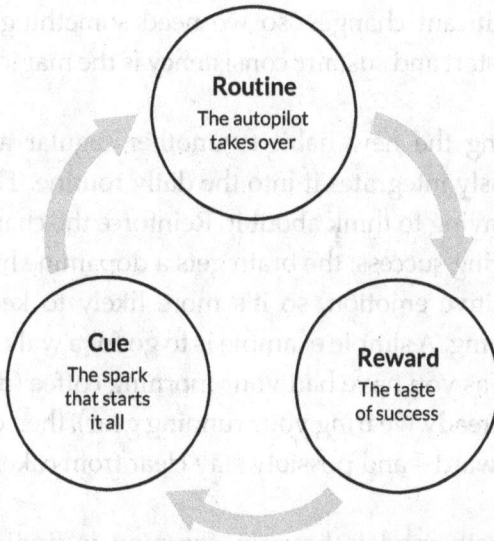

The cue, routine, reward model

This model can be used to introduce a change: keep the cue and reward the same and replace the routine with the desired behaviour. Repetition will reprogramme the brain's automatic response over time, reversing the previous habit. For example, if you are reaching for chocolate too often during the day, keep the cue and reward the same but keep fruit within reach.

Change is easier to achieve by making the new habit as small as possible because it's easier to embed and doesn't rely on willpower.[23] We tend to get discouraged

---

23 BJ Fogg, *Tiny Habits: The small changes that change everything* (Virgin Digital, 2019)

by significant changes, so we need something that's easy to start and sustain; consistency is the magic word.

Attaching the new habit to another regular activity seamlessly integrates it into the daily routine. The aim is not having to think about it. Reinforce the change by celebrating success: the brain gets a dopamine hit with the positive emotion, so it's more likely to keep the habit going. A simple example is to go for a walk or run as soon as you have had your morning coffee (drink it while already wearing your running gear), then choose your reward – and possibly stay clear from cake!

What both models have in common is finding the most effective ways to trick the brain: make it easy and prioritise the emotional rather than rational part of the brain. Willpower doesn't work, as anybody who has tried to create a new habit using willpower alone knows well.

My experience: When introducing a new reward goes wrong

I was visiting a call centre and had the opportunity to observe the most extraordinary (and unwanted) change happen quickly; it was like being in the middle of a behavioural experiment.

Here is the background: the company had many complaints from customers whose calls were unanswered and who were sometimes kept on hold for an hour. It was becoming a big issue, impacting how the company was perceived in the market. There was a trend of customers leaving, thus affecting the bottom line. The department's senior leader wanted to improve this issue, and it was decided that targets had to change to prioritise shorter queue time (ideally none). There was no budget to recruit more staff, so the only change was the reward: a team bonus for shortening the queue.

I was there when the change went live. A screen showed the number of customers in the queue, and it was amazing to see it reducing dramatically and fairly quickly. There were many pats on the shoulder among the project team, but the moment of elation didn't last long – at least until they started looking at the data and discovered that call centre staff on a customer call would hang up the phone even if they had not solved the query, right in the middle of a call. As you may expect, the complaints were now from customers who were angry about having their calls abruptly closed and their issue not being solved.

This happens when you don't test your change intervention and are not careful about what habits you may trigger. To solve one problem, the project team created another because they did not consider people would change their behaviour in a way they didn't expect but could have predicted.

Summary

- The need for psychological safety can't be overestimated. A working environment characterised by uncertainty and fear for the future can cause employees to feel unsafe and stop sharing ideas, asking questions and making mistakes. It is demotivating and it impacts productivity.

- Leaders can role model behaviours that promote psychological safety, in which asking for help and admitting mistakes is accepted. Reward employees for effort, creativity, and stopping projects if they are not expected to achieve the desired outcomes. Encourage challenging conversations.

- Many reasons change can fail are related to fear of the new and comfort in what we know. Several biases are at play – status quo; loss aversion; confirmation, anchoring and optimism bias – each with possible mitigating actions that need to be tailored to the context of the change and organisational culture.

- Sometimes, it all gets a bit too much and we get into cognitive overload or fatigue. Suggestions to avoid this include prioritising change (and removing unnecessary projects), simplifying communications, providing micro-learning and incorporating downtime – all examples of less is more.

- We are social creatures and follow what others do; the group represents safety and security. Leveraging social norms is a powerful technique to drive adoption; rather than telling people what to do, it creates an environment that encourages change. We do this by identifying the behaviours that align with the desired change, leveraging the role of influencers and using norms-based communication techniques.

- Breaking old patterns and creating new habits is central to the success of organisational change because we prioritise the emotional rather than the rational part of the brain. Small habits are more straightforward to adopt. Willpower doesn't work because it takes too much cognitive effort.

FIVE

Clash Of Cultures: When Worlds Collide In Business

We have learnt the importance of behaviours in making change happen, and there may have been the implication that everybody behaves the same. That would be too easy; national and corporate cultures must be considered. Senior executives often underestimate how cultural influences determine the success or failure of a change programme.

The scope of many change programmes spans across borders and departments. Team members are based around the world; there are many opportunities to use this diversity to the best advantage and avoid any pitfalls from cultural clashes.

Why culture matters

Culture is the intangible set of shared values, beliefs and norms that explain how people within a group interact with each other. It exists on many levels: nation, community or organisation. Although not everybody in a group is the same and we should avoid generalisations, some national traits distinguish people of a country. The same applies to organisations: the corporate culture in an investment bank is different from that of a media company. Culture encompasses rituals, symbols, traditions and language. It shapes behaviours, decision-making, conflict resolution and more within an organisation.

Culture also gives a sense of identity to people within that group, creating cohesion. In a company, it is the foundation influencing employees' behaviours and shaping customer experience. A positive culture raises job satisfaction and performance, while a toxic culture leads to conflict, disengagement and high turnover – all bad for the bottom line. Corporate culture shapes brand identity and affects customer loyalty. Some companies have built a loyal customer base using their culture as a pivot, making it a valuable asset. Customer and employee loyalty stretches to attracting and retaining top talent. A positive culture is critical in periods of change because it provides stability and a shared sense of belonging.

There is so much at stake that we want to get the culture right in our change programme.

How culture shapes decisions and outcomes

Two companies consistently come up high in lists of positive culture: Zappos and Southwest Airlines.

EXAMPLE: Zappos – a customer-first culture

Zappos has a customer-focused culture.[24] The company believes the key to achieving that goal is a commitment to happy employees and maintaining an inclusive and innovative working environment. Their recruitment process emphasises cultural fit, and a collective responsibility is to preserve a culture that aligns employee and customer needs.[25]

EXAMPLE: Southwest Airlines – going the extra mile

Southwest Airlines is another company that believes that putting employees first will result in an excellent

---

24 M Mischke, '15 of the Best Company Culture Examples for 2025', *PerformYard* (11 October 2024), www.performyard.com/articles/best-company-culture-examples, accessed 3 April 2025

25 S Patel, '10 Excellent Company Culture Examples for Inspiration,' *Entrepreneur* (26 April 2023), www.entrepreneur.com/growing-a-business/10-examples-of-companies-with-fantastic-cultures/249174, accessed 3 April 2025

customer experience.[26] Employees have the autonomy to go the extra mile if that's going to deliver a better customer experience and so feel part of a larger purpose. Recruitment is key; they prioritise hiring for attitude in addition to skills.

On the other hand, there are companies with toxic cultures who struggle to change. I mentioned Enron earlier as an example of a company whose culture caused its demise. Other examples are Wells Fargo and Uber – the latter seemingly made a successful cultural shift.

EXAMPLE: Wells Fargo – scandals and compensation

Wells Fargo's toxic and pressure-driven culture led to a series of scandals and systemic fraud. In 2016, it emerged that about $1.5 million deposit accounts and more than half a million fake credit card accounts were created over ten years.[27] Sales targets were so aggressive that employees felt they had no other option. The second case concerns the add-on services sold to customers without disclosing they were paid-for services.[28]

26 G Matthews, 'Eight Companies With Amazing Company Culture', *Reward Gateway*, www.rewardgateway.com/uk/blog/eight-companies-with-amazing-company-culture, accessed 3 April 2025
27 M Wilowski, 'Timeline: Wells Fargo's Biggest Legal Settlements,' *Investopedia* (16 May 2023), www.investopedia.com/wells-fargo-timeline-7498799, accessed 3 April 2025
28 'Wells Fargo Scandals Timeline', *Financhill*, https://financhill.com/blog/investing/wells-fargo-scandals-timeline, accessed 3 April 2025

After many years, the practice stopped in 2017, and the company had to return tens of millions of dollars to customers. Over the years, Wells Fargo paid compensation amounting to several billion dollars. It is a heavy price to pay for failing to address evident cultural issues.

EXAMPLE: Uber – unlearning toxic behaviours

Uber grew a reputation for a toxic and aggressive culture, prioritising competition at the expense of standards of conduct.[29] There have also been reports of sexual harassment, workplace hostility and bullying of competitors. This resulted in multiple lawsuits, a loss of trust and a public relations crisis.

The CEO Travis Kalanick was forced to resign in 2017,[30] and under the stewardship of the new CEO Dara Khosrowshahi, things have started to change. The culture has been overhauled through a process of 'unlearning' and the role modelling of ethical leadership.[31] Uber even achieved its first operating profit, a confirmation that a positive culture is good for the bottom line.

---

29   M Isaac, 'Inside Uber's Aggressive, Unrestrained Workplace Culture', *The New York Times* (22 February 2017), www.nytimes.com/2017/02/22/technology/uber-workplace-culture.html, accessed 3 April 2025

30   T Mauri, 'Uber CEO Dara Khosrowshahi Pulled Off a Dramatic Culture Change That Led to Profitability, Here's How It's Done', *Fortune* (3 September 2024), https://fortune.com/2024/09/03/uber-ceo-dara-khosrowshahi-leadership-success-turnaround-how-to-change-company-culture, accessed 3 April 2025

31   B Carson, 'Inside Uber's Effort to Fix Its Culture Through a Harvard-inspired "University"', *Forbes* (3 February 2018), www.forbes.com/sites/bizcarson/2018/02/03/inside-ubers-effort-to-fix-its-culture-through-a-harvard-inspired-university, accessed 3 April 2025

Is it a bad apple or a bad orchard?

The examples above illustrate positive and negative cultures, but what should we do if there is a toxic culture that may derail the change initiative? Or maybe the change is about overhauling an unhealthy culture, so knowing the root cause is important.

The concept of 'bad apple vs. bad orchard' differentiates between individual misconduct and systemic cultural issues. If an individual disrupts the workplace with dishonest, incompetent or toxic behaviour, removing them will restore a positive environment. If, instead, you discover a 'bad orchard', then there's a more complex problem. The negative behaviour is systematic and requires solving deeper issues; otherwise, low morale and unethical behaviours will seriously affect the company.

I have worked in companies where it was easy to see whether it was apple or orchard. The problem is that it's 'easier' to get rid of a bad apple – a rogue trader – but that won't solve the problem. The other problem with the orchard is that a new recruit, mainly if junior, can get easily influenced by the unhealthy environment and – not knowing how to manage a problematic situation and whether to report it – join the bad group.

A toxic workplace is bad for morale and a company's long-term profitability. It needs to change. The first step is to identify the root cause.

Taking it to the next level

This is not just about fixing a problem; creating a positive culture that makes change easier is just as important. In the book *Grit*, Angela Duckworth has a conversation with Dan Chambliss, a sociologist who studies professional swimmers. They discuss the correlation between culture and grit and how you need to join a culture with that characteristic if you want to become more 'gritty'. Likewise, if a leader wants determined and gritty employees, they need to create a gritty culture. Dan concludes that to get grit, 'The hard way is to do it all by yourself. The easy way is to use conformity [...] if you are around a lot of people who are gritty, you are going to act grittier.'[32]

This applies to any cultural value, norm or priority. As a leader, you are best placed to create the culture that will make your company successful through any change.

My experience: Finding balance between global and local

The culture at a British subsidiary of an international company that I worked with was akin to a start-up – nimble and innovative. The employees were enthusiastic and full of drive; there was a real buzz in the

32 A Duckworth, *Grit: Why passion and resilience are the secrets to success* (Vermilion, 2017), p. 289

air. They operated fairly independently from the larger organisation, apart from once a year when they submitted the business plan and forecasting. My role was to help them shift the corporate culture towards more explicit governance and structure to manage the yearly planning cycle.

The first step was to capture how their current activities prepared for the business planning cycle. I wanted the new approach to be as similar as possible to what they were used to, so as to limit the change gap. I also wanted to make the change visible as part of the sense-making exercise, with a poster featuring the process steps to tack on the wall. As I started asking employees about the process, I got different answers regarding both activities and timings. I realised this was going to be more complicated than I'd thought. I mapped the process steps as accurately as possible and played them back among complaints I got wrong, depending on who I talked with. After several revisions, I developed the desired new process and validated it with the requirements of the leading company.

I engaged with people throughout this activity, but I knew the real challenge was yet to come: how to get people to follow the new workflow. I leveraged the support of the CFO and CEO, who assisted the move since they would typically bear the brunt of the challenges from the larger company. Our united front and clear explanation of the benefits got the buy-in of the rest of the board. I made the workflow visible to the teams involved in the business planning; I had my lovely poster with the process steps and star icons to track progress. Employees started to use the new process proactively; they even stuck their photos next to relevant stars. I guess that's an advantage of buzzy start-ups: they develop creative ideas.

The project worked well; it was a difficult journey from resistance, driven by people's attachment to an innovative and independent way of working, to accepting the need for governance. Keeping it simple and as close as possible to their previous working methods helped the change journey run smoothly.

The role of national culture beyond stereotypes

There are two layers of culture most relevant to change: national and corporate. These days, even smaller companies often work across borders. We may think that with globalisation there are no fundamental differences between countries, and with senior execs used to working across borders, national diversity is decreasing, but that's not the case. The dangerous assumption is that there are no differences.

Our national culture influences how we perceive and react to change. Therefore, executives need to modify how they engage and communicate with peers and employees. This overview of the differences most relevant to organisational change is based on research from Trompenaars, Hofstede and Hall.[33,34,35] You may recognise some of these situations from your own experience.

Communication style

I learnt this on my first business trip to the Netherlands. I was used to British politeness, where nobody ever made overt negative comments at meetings. As I was leaving a meeting, some Dutch colleagues bluntly stated that it had been a waste of time, that the chairperson had not prepared properly and that it would be a setback in the subsequent project phases. I was shocked, to say the least. The same situation in the UK would have drawn a comment of, 'Let's have another meeting next week'; here, they refused to be part of the project unless things were fixed first. As I spent more time there, I started to appreciate and embrace the Dutch way. It was useful to know what people thought rather than needing to interpret it.

The Netherlands is an example of a low-context culture (the same as the US and Germany) – communication is direct and explicit. On the flip side, in high-context cultures (i.e. Japan and China), the

33 F Trompenaars and C Hampden-Turner, *Riding the Waves of Culture: Understanding diversity in global business* (McGraw-Hill Education, 1997)
34 G Hofstede and GJ Hofstede, *Cultures and Organizations: Software of the mind,* 2nd edition (McGraw-Hill Education, 2004)
35 ET Hall, *Beyond Culture* (Anchor Books, 1997)

context of non-verbal cues, tone of voice and the relationship between people are as important as the content. You may notice that colleagues from these countries often would not intervene in a conversation unless asked an explicit question.

Implications for change: Coming from a low-context culture and engaging with a high-context one, we need to be particularly careful about non-verbal cues, slow down and include pauses when we talk. Confrontation is avoided; people may imply discomfort but won't express it directly. It's always better to smile than express disagreement. From high to low context, we need to be more explicit, give more details and practise intervening in the conversation, even if not asked.

The importance of power distance

Power distance is an important consideration in how we position a change. People in Asian and Latin American countries tend to be more deferential to authority and less likely to challenge decisions. This is referred to as a high power distance culture. On the other hand, in low power distance countries such as Sweden and Denmark, there is an expectation among employees to be involved in the decision-making. It's easy to see where things can go badly wrong.

Implications for change: The recommendation when leading a change in a high power distance culture is to solicit feedback directly. The perceived initial acceptance can hide resistance and lead to a passive refusal to implement changes later on, even if on the surface all seems well. As for countries with low power distance, we need to involve people from the start.

Facing uncertainty

Uncertainty is inevitable in change; however, different countries approach it differently. Countries with high uncertainty avoidance, such as Germany, Japan, South Korea and Greece, prefer clear rules and processes and feel uncomfortable with ambiguity, risk and unpredictability. On the other hand, low uncertainty avoidance cultures, for example, the US, Singapore, UK and Denmark, are more comfortable with ambiguity and risk, are generally more flexible and are used to working in a dynamic change environment.

Implications for change: Leading a change in countries with high uncertainty avoidance requires detailed plans and setting clear expectations right from the start. Employees need greater reassurance of the steps involved and what the outcome will look like. In countries with low uncertainty avoidance, we can get away with less structured plans and expect less pushback if circumstances change. You can leverage the greater flexibility and openness to risk to test ideas and options, before rolling out to the other countries.

There are more dimensions; however, these three give leaders a good sense of the importance of national cultures when undertaking a change programme. It's important to bring these differences out in the open and make it part of onboarding in any international project.

Before starting an international project, research other cultures. It's useful to incorporate fun activities at the start of a programme to ensure people know how to communicate and solve tricky situations with colleagues abroad or in other functions.

Subcultures in business: Why one size doesn't fit all

There are two layers of corporate culture to consider: overall and functional subcultures.

Overall subcultures

Corporate culture is a shared set of values, beliefs and behaviours – the organisation's personality driving how employees interact with each other, their customers and other stakeholders. One standard change mishap can occur when a leader joining a new company wants to drive the same transformation he did in his previous one. Although the prospect of replicating a previous major success is tempting – and likely he was hired based on that achievement – the reality may not be as expected.

EXAMPLE: J.C. Penney – Ron Johnson's attempt to recreate success[36,37]

Ron Johnson created the iconic Apple stores, revolutionising the retail experience with a sleek design and excellent customer experience, leading to a massive increase in revenue. When he joined J.C. Penney as CEO, he sought to recreate the same experience and expected a similar revenue increase.

The corporate culture at J.C. Penney was different: traditional, family-friendly and hierarchical. It reflected the profile of its price-sensitive customer base, which is used to promotions and discounts. These two corporate cultures were at opposite ends of the scale, so when Ron Johnson started to refurbish stores to create an upscale and sleek experience – and removed the all-important discount vouchers – the backlash was quick among staff and customers, sales dropped quickly and he was ousted after seventeen months.

---

36 S Denning, 'J.C.Penney: Was Ron Johnson's Strategy Wrong?', *Forbes* (9 April 2013), www.forbes.com/sites/stevedenning/2013/04/09/ j-c-penney-was-ron-johnsons-strategy-wrong, accessed 23 May 2025

37 B Tuttle, 'The 5 Big Mistakes That Led to Ron Johnson's Ouster at JC Penney', *Time* (9 April 2013), https://business.time.com/2013/04/09/ the-5-big-mistakes-that-led-to-ron-johnsons-ouster-at-jc-penney, accessed 23 May 2025

Replicating previous successes may be tempting, but this only works when the culture and organisational context are similar.

Functional subcultures

Functional subcultures are distinctive groups within any organisation, shaped by their particular roles and areas of expertise. Each subculture develops its norms, values and rules based on how it interacts with other parts of the organisation. They have shared characteristics and styles: the marketing team focuses on creativity and customer perceptions, and the finance team focuses on accuracy and compliance. These differences are valuable and necessary, but they may cause problems when we need to lead the whole organisation through a change. Groups will have different expectations and communications have to be targeted to their preferences.

Leaders are uniquely positioned at the company's top to see how the components fit together and influence reactions and actions through their top team. Change leaders are well placed to bring functions together. We often underestimate the importance of achieving a shared language, but we fall prey to biases and misunderstandings without it. In change, rational arguments are not compelling; instead, we need to understand the people's natural preferences and emotional reactions. Bringing together sales and engineering representatives in the same change project must consider balancing the former high-energy, results-driven preferences with the engineers focusing on precision and analytical thinking, where often the drive is solving complex problems.

These subcultures respond to change initiatives differently, and we need to consider this when we plan how to engage and communicate with them.

My experience: Marketing and technology – two teams separated by language

As part of a project in the technology sector, I was asked to bring together teams across marketing and technology and identify solutions to improve collaboration. It seemed fun and easy compared with other work I did. So little I knew!

At the first joint meeting, I had about twenty people in the room – a mix from the two departments. I also had a loose agenda, since I was not sure what to expect and wanted to use this first meeting as an introduction to get a sense of the working environment and practices; there would be the opportunity to get into the root cause and explore any issues at a later stage. After introductions, I asked about their expectations on this project to improve teamwork and their thoughts on what collaboration meant to them. It was like letting them loose, each on their own soapbox. There were so many complaints about the other teams: they didn't understand requests and never provided the correct information. Among all this, I started picking up jargon and – in the short gaps in the monologues – questions such as, 'What do you mean by that?' It was like watching a chaotic sitcom (I started to fancy popcorn until I realised it was my meeting, so I had to bring order!).

I decided to choose one of the comments and delve into it as if it were a case study. It soon became apparent how different the language in the two departments was; as expected, they had their own jargon, but even the same 'normal' English words were used in other contexts and with different meanings. We started picking words or sentences and discussing them until we reached a shared understanding. We continued for the rest of the meeting, and it started becoming fun. I could see the high level of engagement among the participants, which was rewarding.

It was an eye-opener; I learnt how language can cause misunderstandings and barriers, and it revealed how important accurate communication is.

My experience: The cultural cracks that sink M&As

I once made a cultural assessment of the acquisition by a British company of a smaller Italian one. The question was whether the national and customer service subcultures impacted the acquisition's success and how to manage the integration better. I collected data at three organisational levels in both companies: interviews with senior leaders, focus groups with middle managers and a questionnaire for the broader employee base.

The interviews were useful in understanding the drivers of this acquisition, the expected benefits and personal experiences. Talking with executives on both sides, I had an insight into the reciprocal expectations. Unlike many M&As, there was an existing relationship between the two companies. Therefore, it was easier to develop shared understanding and trust, even if the loss of independence was acutely felt. I can only imagine how fraught things can get in a hostile takeover.

There were cultural differences at the national level. For the Italian team, forging relationships felt necessary, while meeting outside the office for a coffee or a meal was considered a waste of time by the British executives, who were more pragmatic and direct in their approach. Here was an opportunity to find a win-win, which would have been easy for both sides but was missed. Being Italian, I naturally prefer getting to know people; having an informal chat with someone helps me learn their opinions more easily and quickly than at a desk in the office. We often achieve more significant progress during an impromptu, informal chat than through emails sent over several weeks.

The focus groups provided a wealth of insights on corporate culture and subcultures. I used the Cultural Web model by Gerry Johnson and Kevan Scholes,[38] which captures the distinctive culture of a company across six interrelated elements that influence assumptions and practices within the organisation:

1. Stories

2. Symbols

3. Power structures

4. Organisational structures

5. Control systems

6. Rituals and routines

I asked people to describe the two companies' cultures across these six dimensions to extract their paradigm. The significant finding was how close the customer service subcultures were – more significant than national culture differences – which I was not expecting. The implication is that once you overcome the language barrier, the collaboration between functions is easier, with the opportunity to share resources and work to support international clients.

The questionnaire asked about both types of culture, with a primary interest in organisational structure and

---

38 G Johnson, K Scholes and R Whittington, *Fundamentals of Strategy* (Prentice Hall, 2009)

leadership style. As expected, the Italian company – like in many Mediterranean countries – was more hierarchical. There was more respect for authority, and employees expected direction from the top, which they would follow. In this situation, giving people more autonomy and freedom to decide can backfire, leaving both sides waiting and waiting. Missing these cues is easy; they may seem small, but they have remarkably high impacts. In this case, it added several weeks of delay: one side was waiting for direction, while the other was wondering why people were not making any progress.

Using the Cultural Web model to compare two companies

This is a fictitious example of how the culture web can identify cultural differences.

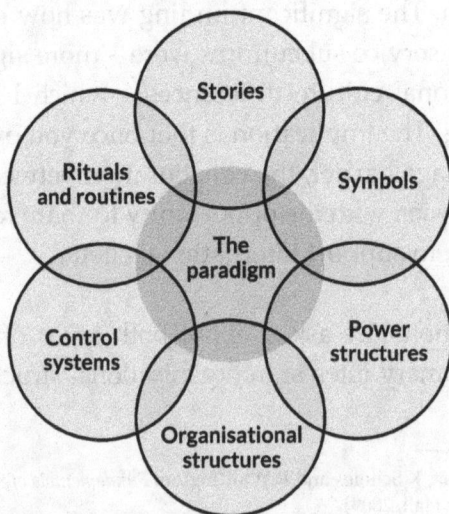

	Company A	Company B
Paradigm (core beliefs and assumptions)	Amazing ideas can come from anyone Speed and adaptability are key – we move fast, test often and learn from mistakes Collaboration is at the heart of everything we do	We have a chain of command, and decisions go through the proper channels Each department focuses on its own responsibilities; we rarely collaborate across teams We have worked this way for years, there's no need to change what we know
Stories	One of our first big products came from a junior developer's idea The CEO worked alongside the team the whole weekend	Our CEO made a bold decision years ago that shaped the company, and we still follow that vision Once, a junior employee tried to push a new idea, but it never got past the management layers

	Company A	Company B
Rituals and routines	Every Friday, we have a company-wide demo to showcase that week's developments We kick off projects with brainstorming: everybody is encouraged to contribute	Every decision requires several levels of approval; things take time to progress The purpose of meetings is to report upwards; we don't discuss new ideas
Symbols	Our office is open-plan. Everyone sits together, from interns to the CEO Whiteboards and sticky notes cover our walls because we're always ideating	Corner offices make it clear who the senior leaders are Titles and job levels matter a lot; that's how people introduce themselves
Organisational structures	Teams self-organise around projects; there are no rigid departments Managers are more like coaches; they are there to help people grow not control them	You have to go through the proper hierarchy to get things approved; you get into trouble if you bypass your manager New joiners learn quickly that knowing the right leaders is the best way to get things done

	Company A	Company B
Control systems	We don't have KPIs; we focus on learning and iterating based on real-time feedback We track success based on impact, not hours worked	We use strict KPIs to track performance; the priority is meeting targets Employees are expected to be at their desks during their working hours
Power structures	Decisions are made by those closest to the problem Anyone can challenge the status quo; influence is based on your ideas, not job title	Decisions are made by leaders, and employees are expected to follow them You need executive sponsorship to move forward a project

M&A failures: Missing the cultural boat

Many M&As fail, and many of these failures are due to missing the culture boat. It is an essential, not a nice to have.

EXAMPLE: Daimler-Benz and Chrysler – a failed merger

A frequently cited example of a failed merger is between Daimler-Benz and Chrysler in 1998. Valued at $36 billion, it was hailed as a 'merger of equals' between two major car manufacturers to create a global producer of both luxury and mass-market vehicles.[39]

Once the deal was signed and the real work started, the first cracks appeared in national and corporate culture. On one side, the structured and hierarchical German company and, on the other, Chrysler's American informal and risk-taking culture. The functional priorities also differed; Daimler-Benz was engineer-driven, while Chrysler was cost-focused. The clashes happened at all levels, from executive to operational. The merger failed to deliver the planned synergies and cost savings, and was de-merged in 2007 when Daimler sold 80% of its stake.[40]

Sometimes, keeping an acquired company separate is the most appropriate option. This was the case with Google's acquisition of YouTube in 2006, Amazon's acquisition of Zappos in 2009 and Facebook's acquisition of Instagram in 2012. The acquired companies in these examples have been more successful operating under the parent company than before, and seem to have maintained their independence. This approach is a successful blend of enabling innovation while benefiting from investment from the parent company.

39 G Wearden, 'From $35bn to $7.4bn in Nine Years', *The Guardian* (14 May 2007), www.theguardian.com/business/2007/may/14/motoring.lifeandhealth, accessed 4 April 2025

40 M Milner, 'Private Equity Group Takes 80% Stake in Chrysler to End Merger Nightmare', *The Guardian* (15 May 2007), www.theguardian.com/business/2007/may/15/motoring.privateequity, accessed 4 April 2025

M&A failures amount to millions of dollars in losses: not making enough of the expected savings, inability to integrate resources and escalating costs. Ideally, leaders need to instigate a cultural assessment before the M&A decision. This is often not possible as the initial discussions are secret; however, the sooner after that, the better. It will save time, money and headaches later on.

My experience: Cultural missteps – a quick round-the-world trip

Below is a brief round-up of my insights from leading international change programmes. These are just a few examples of seemingly minor cultural differences that can significantly impact a change programme. Even executives who have worked across borders for many years can easily miss some of them.

The tall poppies syndrome

It was my first time working in Australia, and I sensed some resistance from the client leadership and my Australian colleagues. I sensed some underlying criticism, more so than is expected in a change project (you are rarely the most loved person). I couldn't figure out why, until a kind colleague explained: I was too much of a 'show off'. What I considered confidence (and something expected in an external consultant there to advise clients) was a discouraged trait in a culture where humility was more important. Humility is good, but cutting down tall poppies can stifle ambition and innovation.

Employees won't ask the manager for help

It was an international project, and we were preparing the comms to support a change in HR processes that would impact all employees. We provided more information to managers, and the message to employees was to 'ask your line manager if you need help or have any questions'.

We were reviewing the translation with the country leads for China and Hong Kong when they told me the message would not work there, and we had to change it. I discovered that in those countries and others in the region, employees hesitate to ask their managers for help as it can be seen as an admission of incompetence or perceived as a sign of weakness. This can be explained by the high power distance dimension we covered earlier and the importance of face-saving.

Face-saving

I have found this especially significant in India and some Asian countries. In these cultures, avoiding public embarrassment is particularly important, especially regarding the potential loss of respect and one's standing within the team. This means people avoid admitting delays, mistakes and doubts, and direct confrontation.

Working with Indian colleagues, I would be told an action was completed or progressing well, only to learn at the last moment and indirectly that there was a problem, which meant I had to face an annoyed client with apologies and a hastily created recovery plan. I learnt to manage these situations by carefully questioning the progress made and greater reliance on hints and non-verbal cues.

Practical steps to get culture right

Resistance to change due to cultural differences can be an opportunity to revisit your own culture. An assessment or audit before the change programme will highlight potential sources of resistance. This data gives information as to whether there is a need to define, revamp or refine the current culture. Ideally, these activities must occur before, or at least in parallel with, the change programme. Recognising that differences exist means we can learn about them and act. Signs of cultural mismatch are similar to any resistance to change and include high turnover, widespread non-compliance and informal undermining of change.

Here are the steps to manage organisational impacts from cultural diversity more effectively:

1. **Define your desired culture.** This applies to cases when you want to trigger a significant shift; for example, the company is losing market share because competitors are developing better

products. In this case, you want a culture that is more innovative, collaborative and ready to take risks. If the gap between today and the future is wide, it may not be a manageable undertaking, but it is necessary. It requires careful planning and is a long-term change implementation.

2. **Culture audit.** This is essential for significant changes, such as M&As, new operating models or international expansions, and is useful in most other change situations. The aim is to gain an in-depth understanding of the culture of two organisations or the impacted functions within a company. Only by identifying the gaps and impacts can evidence-driven interventions be determined. People won't fit in the wrong mould, and differences in values and beliefs will come back to bite you. Tools such as the Cultural Web (see above) are useful to reveal hidden and unconscious – but often powerful – cultural elements.

3. **Storytelling.** Emphasise values that can be easily shared across cultures, using stories to bring them to life. Values such as innovation, collaboration and autonomy can easily apply to any function. I suggest developing stories and sharing them consistently until they become part of the standard way of working. Have stories that span the before and after change to support the transition. If a new value will be of benefit, seek even a small story to bring it to light while dispelling potential concerns.

4. **Monitor cultural alignment.** Measures and data are the foundations to assess the impact of any change. Tools such as the Cultural Web, surveys and sentiment analysis give you the data to track cultural shifts. You can then maintain the same activities or tweak them to align the change actions to the end goals.

The common wisdom is that culture is difficult to change. Shared values, beliefs, attitudes and behaviours that have grown organically over many years cannot be easily overhauled. It is not impossible, though. We can start with an audit, and by defining the desired culture, we can then make small and consistent changes to achieve a cultural shift. It will be slow, but it will happen.

Summary

- We can observe and assess culture at national, corporate or group levels. Understanding an organisation's rituals, symbols, traditions and language gives us the tools to implement change more effectively.

- Corporate culture influences brand identity and impacts customer experience. A positive culture provides stability and a shared sense of belonging in periods of change.

- A toxic culture may be centred on an individual instance of misconduct or there may be systemic issues. It's essential to distinguish between a 'bad apple' and a 'bad orchard' as they require different interventions. The situation of a bad orchard is more complex to solve with several behavioural change interventions.

- Understanding national differences is essential for companies operating across borders and can maximise results. Beyond stereotypes, there are differences in how people communicate, relate to authority and deal with uncertainty.

- Functional subcultures are distinctive groups within any organisation. Their areas of expertise shape their character, language and how they interact with other functions.

- M&As are a perfect example of why understanding culture matters to people, and the bottom line. Many fail to achieve the planned benefits because the cultures won't integrate. Leaders need to instigate a cultural assessment as early as possible to evaluate risks and options.

- A cultural assessment in advance of a change programme allows the identification of potential sources of resistance, which is useful to refine the current culture. Designing the desired culture is not quick or easy but has pervasive, long-term effects. By making small and consistent changes, we can achieve a noticeable cultural shift.

PART THREE

LESSONS FROM FAILURE: HOW TO BUILD A CULTURE OF SUCCESS

SIX

When Words Fail: Navigating The Pitfalls Of Communication

The aim of communication is to ensure employees understand the purpose and value of the change, what it means for them and what they are expected to do differently. Every change project singles out communication as essential to a successful implementation. When you ask employees about their understanding of a change, they often say they don't know what it is about and what it means for them. The onus is on leaders to ensure employees understand and act upon the message.

We frequently communicate too much content, and our messages are often not targeted to the audience. The challenge we should set is to describe the programme in the most straightforward language that would fit on a postcard.

This chapter covers key elements for successful communication: setting the vision, selling the change and the power of storytelling. It concludes with how to spot signs of communication breakdown and solutions.

My experience: A case of communication failure

I learnt the most about communications in this programme, working with an exec team to prepare for a significant change announcement, including the vision for this change, the why and what. We encouraged them to start from a blank slate and strip away preconceived ideas of how they have done it before. We wanted to set the language and tone for the whole programme.

Once we had a good first version, I stripped away jargon and business speak that often confounds communication, ensuring the message was clear, concise and accessible. I was proud of it: the narrative was clear and relatable. It outlined what the change would look and feel like and what it would mean for the company and its employees. It also had a high-level plan of key activities. The details would come later once we had more inputs, but we had a solid foundation for now.

We were ready for the launch. This is when all the preparation would pay off – or so I thought. We did our due diligence, including a dry run with a small group to gather feedback and refine our message. I soon learnt that even the best-prepared presentations can sometimes miss the mark in ways you never expected.

The day of the launch arrived. We had secured a great venue, and over 300 employees were attending. The content was ready, and I had prepped the executive who would present. I knew the material inside out and was genuinely excited about the message we were about to deliver. As the presentation began, I positioned myself halfway down the room to observe the presenter and the audience.

The executive delivered the presentation flawlessly. The slides were clear, the message was strong and the Q&A session that followed was handled with ease. Everything was going according to plan. As the session ended and people began to file out of the room, I listened to their comments. The initial feedback you overhear gives you a quick gauge of how well the message landed.

That's when I heard it – the first comment that stopped me in my tracks: 'There's no plan. He didn't tell us when this is all going to happen.' I was shocked. How could they not know the plan? We had laid it out clearly in the presentation. I had written those slides myself and knew exactly where the timeline was discussed. Before I could process that, I heard another comment: 'I don't really understand the point of doing this.'

I was dumbfounded. How could they not understand the point? We had spent weeks crafting a message that explained the 'why' behind the change, the benefits and the impacts. It was all there – on the slides, in the speech, in the answers to their questions. Somehow, the message hadn't landed.

Those brief exchanges as people walked out of the room were pivotal in my understanding of communications. They taught me a lesson that I carry with me to this day: never assume that just because you've said something, people have heard, understood and internalised it. Until that day, I naively believed that if you told people something, they would automatically understand it, but communication isn't that simple. It's not enough to deliver information – you must ensure the message is received, understood and remembered.

This realisation changed my approach to presenting change. From then on, I ensured key messages were repeated, reinforced and rephrased in different ways to ensure they stuck. I started delivering the same information in alternative ways, and I began using multiple channels to communicate – emails, follow-up meetings, one-on-one discussions – anything to ensure the message was clear and everyone was on the same page.

I also became more aware of the nuances of communication. People don't absorb information passively, they interpret it through their filters, biases and experiences. What is crystal clear to us might confuse others, depending on their perspective and how they process information.

The learning from this programme remains a valuable reminder that the success of a change initiative isn't about having a grand vision or a solid plan but how well you communicate that vision and plan to the people who need to buy into it. Communication is a two-way street, and even the best-prepared presentations can go awry if we don't connect with the audience. Don't just assume they'll understand it – make sure they do.

How to create a vision people believe in

More than in any other business situation, the uncertainty of change means that visualising the final destination becomes essential. That's the purpose of the vision.

There is a caveat: the vision in our head may make perfect sense to us, but other people may not connect with it. The journey towards the future state is uncertain; we ask people to believe in something that is still intangible, so we need to help them relate to the vision and gain their trust. To create a vision, you will need to do the following:

Engage stakeholders

Have a cross-section of people, in addition to the programme sponsor and leads, including the heads of the departments most impacted by the change and others likely to influence the outcome.

Should we include anyone who's against the change? It depends. If they are likely to be disruptive in the meeting, then I would exclude them. We don't want to detract from the experience of the others. If they are highly opinionated but happy to listen to others and contribute, then definitely yes.

Communicate the vision

Despite sounding obvious, I have seen leaders presenting the vision once, but it's only with regular repetition that the vision becomes understood among employees. Their interest and engagement need to be triggered and maintained over time. Leaders have become familiar with the vision, developing and discussing it with their team; repetition contributes to sense-making and remembering it. Employees need the same experience, which minimal exposure can't achieve.

My rule of thumb is to present the vision three times in the first three months – although not tested, it's easy to remember. The language needs to be simple and clear, with no jargon. Consistency is essential when presented by a range of executives.

Communications are shaped by leaders based on their perspective; however, employees perceive them based on their own different perspectives. At the simplest level, a leader message, 'This change will save money,' can be perceived as, 'I am going to lose my job.' As shown in the figure below, the messaging needs to start from the 'me' in the middle to ensure it is understood.

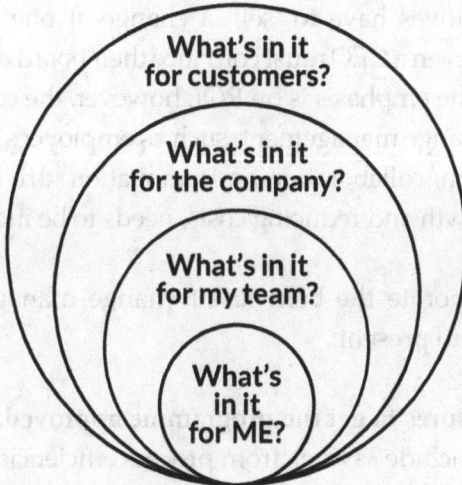

What's in it for customers?

What's in it for the company?

What's in it for my team?

What's in it for ME?

Change narrative

Measure how the vision is perceived

Sometimes, we skip this vital step, as I learnt in the case above. Even the best-crafted vision and case for change can fall flat if it doesn't connect with people. Preparation tends to be inward-looking; the audience won't think and feel in the same way and will have their own biases and expectations. A dry run is useful to test reactions and adjust. The group should be diverse, and I ask for feedback individually, not as a group, to remove the herd effect. Other options are listening to comments as people leave the room or using tools to record immediate feedback via smartphones.

The boardroom pitch: Making the case for change

All executives have to 'sell' a change at one time or another; even a CEO must convince their board or shareholder. The emphasis is on ROI; however, the contribution of change management, such as employees' greater motivation, collaboration and innovation, driving revenue growth and reducing costs, needs to be included.

To incorporate the benefits of change management, we need to present:

- **Measures to get the programme approved.** These can include savings from process efficiencies (change contribution is making sure people adhere to new processes) and an increase in revenue from a more motivated and thus productive workforce. There may also be reduced turnover costs, productivity gains from greater collaboration and costs avoided from project delays.

- **Research.** This is valuable but is to be used with caution. Relying on benchmarking what competitors are doing will get you to where they are, but you want to leap ahead. The same applies to customer research; people answer based on what they know now and what they could have. We all know the famous Henry Ford quote, 'If I had asked my customers what they wanted, they would have said a faster horse.'

  The most useful research is on how the change can be implemented. I was working with a client seeking to implement a time and attendance system among tech-adverse teams, and we explored companies in a diverse set of industries with similar challenges and identified helpful ideas.

- **Risks.** A programme is unlikely to achieve the expected benefits without change management interventions. I have worked with executives with a strong belief in the importance of change and others who chose to save money by skipping change activities. I later learnt that they struggled to achieve the planned improvements. I think this may be my own quote: 'If you implement a system people don't use, you are just left with an expensive toy.'

Insights in human behaviours help influence decision-makers and secure funding for the project. Robert Cialdini's research in the art of influence and persuasion is invaluable.[41] Among his principles, these are the ones I have found most useful when seeking board approval:

- **Consistency.** Align the project with previous decisions made by the board, and reference how the commitment to the planned outcome of the project (i.e. innovation, cost savings, efficiency) relates to their strategy. Make it as easy as possible to see these relationships. Senior executives have multiple demands on their time, therefore clarity and conciseness are key requirements.

- **Scarcity.** This is about creating a sense of urgency. I have seen some boards having a desire for change, only for reluctance to rise as they get closer to a decision. This is understandable if a decision requires millions of dollars in investment or a shift in direction. Hesitance and inaction can also be expensive. Sometimes, there is a small window of opportunity to benefit from a competitive market advantage. Large organisations have many stakeholders who want

---

41 RB Cialdini, *Influence: The psychology of persuasion* (Harper Business, 2012) and RB Cialdini, *Pre-Suasion: A revolutionary way to influence and persuade* (Cornerstone Digital, 2016)

to be part of the decision, but their approval is not necessary; unfortunately, their involvement causes delays. Emphasise how scarce the window of opportunity is.

- **Liking.** It seems obvious, but we don't spend enough time and effort in forging strong relationships with decision-makers. People are more open to requests from those they know and like. Finding an ally on the board and developing a connection is valuable, as is tailored engagement with individual stakeholders before seeking group consensus. These networks of influence are valuable for informally discussing the change programme with a senior stakeholder. It is also worth considering how the programme aligns with any personal goals of the decision-makers, such as sustainability or community impacts, as they can be another enabler in getting a sign-off.

Now you have the programme approved, it's time to get the support of all the other stakeholders and employees impacted.

Facts tell, stories sell: The power of storytelling

Storytelling is the best communication method, but we don't use it enough and therefore miss the opportunity to create emotional connections with employees.

Humans are primed to listen to stories – that's how we learn about the world around us – and they are much easier to remember. The first TED Talk I ever listened to from ten, maybe fifteen, years ago – 'My Stroke of Insight' by Jill Bolte Taylor – had so vivid an impression on me that is still imprinted in my mind.[42] I was mesmerised by the power of her storytelling.

Telling memorable stories is more complex than it seems and requires practice. When we see people on stage telling a story flawlessly, we don't realise that it took a lot of practice, feedback and even more practice. If you feel you are not yet an excellent storyteller, practice is the only option. Here is what you need to get started:

- **Purpose.** 'What do you want to achieve with the story?' It may be inspiring or persuasive. It needs to connect the audience emotionally, which is essential when seeking support for change either from the board or from employees.

- **Relatable characters.** The character in the story – it may be you or someone else – needs to be relatable. When people identify with a character, it develops trust. I remember a town hall announcement of job cuts, where the CEO wore an expensive suit. You could sense the barrier forming, as people could not relate. Relatability

---

42 J Bolte Taylor, 'My Stroke of Insight | Jill Bolte Taylor | TED', www.youtube.com/watch?v=UyyjU8fzEYU, accessed 4 April 2025

can be about the topic or how the presenter comes across.

- **Emotional connection.** This drives attention and ensures people remember the story. Any feeling, from inspiration to excitement, transmits empathy and draws the audience, who feel compelled to share the experience with others. The connection sustains the change over time.

- **Tension.** Good stories have conflict and resolution; from *Little Red Riding Hood* to *The Gruffalo*, we notice how enthralled children are. We want the audience to be engaged and on the edge of their seats, waiting to know how the drama is solved.

- **Simplicity.** Audiences need to be able to easily follow the story. If it is over-complicated with unnecessary information, it causes confusion. Steve Jobs' product launches are a perfect example; there wasn't anything technical and it was all about the user experience.

- **Credibility.** Building trust with the audience is essential; the story must be a genuine personal experience or one that resonates with the audience.

- **The start and end are the most critical times.** Engage the audience immediately so they want to keep listening, and conclude by leaving a lasting, powerful impression. You want the message to stay with them.

Stories help people relate to the change and what actions they were responsible for. Whatever story you use, it needs to be meaningful and relatable.

My experience: Boxes or data – Cloud migration is like moving house

Leading the move to the Cloud and working virtually in two companies seemed like easy projects. After all, what's not to like about having access to documents and information wherever you are? I soon discovered I was naïve. I was expecting connectivity concerns and people unwilling to trust colleagues not to mess up their documents.

The most significant barrier was cleaning up data. Something I barely considered before it became a major blocker.

One client was a large and traditional organisation of about 20,000 employees, many of whom used PCs and generally had limited digital skills. Documents were stored locally. In some instances, for the past twenty years, nothing had been ever deleted, with numerous versions and occasional backups. And, of course, the same documents and versions were stored in multiple PCs. The other client was a sleek and creative company with fewer than 100 members of staff but lots of high-definition photos and videos, which I soon realised were taking up much space.

With high amounts of data stored, the mantra 'garbage in, garbage out' had never been more relevant. This was not about being tidy; data storage is expensive, and companies want efficiency and lower costs. Moreover, there are regulations on how long to keep documents.

Part of my role was to convince people they had to clean up (and delete) data before moving to the Cloud. I knew that just telling them would not work, and I could not refer to the Cloud too much (early communications stated how much space there is in the Cloud; with hindsight, that was a mistake, not a selling point!) or talk about gigabytes and megabytes. Instead, I spoke and shared stories about decluttering before a house move; after all, who wants to pay for two lorries rather than one to move clutter from the old to the new house? What about the nuisance of getting to the new house and filling it up with stuff you don't actually want?

These stories were the core of my communications and encouraged people to share their horror house-move tales. On a more practical level, I created a schedule and checklist for sorting through data, just as we have when moving house. I gained their commitment to using them and line managers' support to track progress and report back.

How messages are lost in translation

There are common reasons for communication breakdown, and recognising them can prevent jeopardising the success of the change.

Misalignment between purpose and delivery

This happens when the leadership team is not in complete agreement and has not internalised the vision and direction of the change. Executives present their 'interpretation' of the vision and change journey, or they modify the message to fit the priorities within their department and make it more palatable to their employees.

Even if the message does not deviate from what should be the agreed vision, it may be enough to cause confusion and uncertainty. As we have seen, an employee already feeling the uncertainty and fear surrounding the change will seize any word or impression, confirming it is right to be fearful.

Cultural mismatch

Employees may automatically resist a change if there is an inconsistency between the company's culture – its shared norms and values – and the purpose of the change. This is an emotional rather than rational reaction and, therefore, is more complex to manage (Chapters 4 and 5 explored this topic in more depth).

I see this happening in reorganisations, outsourcing, and when asking people to consider volunteer redundancy. Suppose the company norms and values have been about kindness, compassion and trust, and employees are facing a change whose purpose is to move them to another company or face redundancy. In that case, there is tension and an emotional reaction. Communication will break down because of that mismatch and the outcome is felt more strongly in a company with those values.

Different journey phases

Leaders will always be one or more steps ahead in the change journey, purely because they instigate and shape the vision for the change so they know what's happening and why. The communication breakdown happens if they forget this difference and talk with employees as if they were in the same phase of the change journey as them. I notice this when leaders express their surprise, and sometimes frustration, with employees not getting on board with the change. It takes time for people to make sense of what's happening – it happened to leaders earlier. Moreover, they have more significant say and control over the change programme.

My experience: When corporate values clash with reality

I was working on a change project that involved reorganisation and redundancies. The company's culture was to care for and value employee contributions and personal development. Unfortunately, it was in a difficult financial position, and the company had to reduce costs. It was the first time they had let anybody go, and the leadership team didn't have the expertise to manage this difficult change.

My first task was to help them come to terms with the change, the new organisational structure and the impact on their own roles. They were at the denial and anger stage of the change curve (see Chapter 3), and I believed they should not communicate with employees until they had reached acceptance.

We then started developing the change and communications approach. I set the expectation that there would be a lot of resistance; the inconsistency between their values and culture and making people redundant was undeniable. I set the expectation of a gloomy scenario and hoped it would not be as bad. Moreover, there was no budget for getting a specialist company to support people with job search and CV surgeries, so we set something up internally between the HR team, some managers and myself.

The day of the announcement came, and the reaction was as bad as expected. We had weeks of talking with distressed employees, everybody walking on egg-shells. Some people underestimate how emotionally draining this is. We made it through, and employees found the job search and CV surgeries valuable, which I recommend in these situations.

There was a big mistake, though; we were so focused on the people who were made redundant that we forgot the 'survivors'. These employees also felt the strain of the situation, and their morale dropped considerably. The leading cause was the dissonance of working for a 'caring' company that made people redundant, and that their turn may come one day. It was a useful lesson and something I've sought to avoid since then. As for how to manage the disconnect between values and the change purpose, there is no easy solution. The most beneficial option is to have a support mechanism in place to help people move on.

Solutions to getting your message understood

For communication to resonate with people, the type of change and culture need to be considered. These are solid foundations that apply to any change programme comms.

Test the message

To avoid misalignment between the message and its delivery, I encourage executives to discuss the purpose, vision and benefits of the change until they are clear and there is complete agreement. The commitment to consistent communication is essential; executives may tweak the content for their team while maintaining the core message. A Case for Change pack is a valuable reference document with all the key information, a script of key points and more detailed content to share after the presentation. It's essential to test the message.

As per the earlier story, never assume that a message that makes sense to us will be understood and well received by others. Even a dry run may not iron out all the issues, but it removes many of them.

Make it two-way

We all get annoyed when we want to raise a question or complaint and a company makes it difficult to do so. Employees experience the same frustration if there are no mechanisms to ask questions or interact with leaders and the project team. As we saw in Chapter 4, people don't respond well when told what to do. They want to be engaged, so it's essential to set up the means for people to connect and ask questions.

This issue was apparent when working with an experienced and capable leader who was reluctant to interact with employees. Her leadership style had always been aloof, and she was more at ease sitting in her office than walking the floor. It was a long time ago, and most workplaces are more informal these days. The office layout plays an important role and can be used effectively to encourage communication and other positive behavioural changes. If you have – or maybe recognise yourself in this description – a leader who is ill at ease with walking the floor, there are two options. The first is a journey starting with self-awareness and choosing whether to change and how. Since this is unlikely to be a quick fix, the second, more short-term option is to nominate someone else to be on the front of the change. A leader doesn't need to be the figurehead; delegating to the relevant person can be more effective.

Do not assume people remember

We may explain something once and expect the other person to remember and make sense of it, but that's not the reality. We filter information and connect with whatever sounds familiar (often because we have heard it before). We all show this trait, and since our attention span is getting shorter, we seek brief, punchy messages. Within this context, during a thirty-minute presentation with lots of content, we can expect people to remember two to three concepts. (Unless we are distracted. In that case, maybe it's zero.)

Communication is not a one-off event, and many programmes fail to establish a connection with employees for this reason. Repetition is essential, since we remember more easily something that sounds familiar: something in our brain clicks with recognition and leaves an imprint in our memory. There is no need for the content to be identical. However, the ideas and concepts need to be and thus resonate with the audience. Visual communication is essential; having a programme logo or a recognisable framework helps people connect with the message and purpose.

Transparency

I was unsure whether to include this, but having just written about not making assumptions, I feel I have to. People tend to assume the worst if there is a void. A change is already a time of uncertainty, and the perception that the leadership may withhold information – especially not share the purpose, or 'why' – creates distrust, with all its negative consequences. It's not always possible to have all the information before a change announcement, especially for the most sensitive changes such as M&As and reorganisations.

An open and brave leadership style is essential. There are many leaders with high levels of empathy who can share bad news or say, 'I don't know yet,' if the outcomes are unclear. They have the capability to develop trust among employees and carry them through times of uncertainty.

Summary

- People interpret content through their own filters, biases and experiences. What's clear to us may be utterly opaque to others. Never assume that telling something implies that people know what you mean.

- The uncertainty of change means the destination is essential; it is for leaders to share the future state with employees and help them connect with it, developing trust along the way. We need consistent communication and to measure how it is perceived over time.

- Executives have to 'sell' the need for change. This includes the benefits of change interventions to achieve high levels of adoption through employees' motivation, collaboration and innovation, driving revenue growth and reducing costs.

- There are three persuasion techniques we can leverage to secure funding: consistency by aligning the project with previous decisions, creating a sense of urgency through scarcity in a competitive marketplace, and liking – forging strong relationships with decision-makers.

- Storytelling creates emotional connections with employees. Telling memorable stories takes practice and some essential ingredients.

You want to achieve relatable stories to build trust and create an emotional connection.

- The most common causes of communication breakdown are misalignment between purpose and delivery, cultural tension if the planned change is inconsistent with the company's norms and values, and misunderstanding if leaders and employees are at different stages in their change journey.

- Solutions to better communications include testing the message and creating mechanisms for two-way interactions with employees.

- Never assume people remember communications or pay attention to a whole presentation; instead, focus on repetition to grow familiarity with the content to ensure the message lands. Be transparent, since people veer towards the worst-case scenario in periods of uncertainty.

SEVEN

Change Without Measurement Is Guesswork

D ecisions require quality, not quantity, of data, and often, we have more of the latter. Data is useful if it is both accurate and relevant. It is not enough, though, as data is open to interpretation, so we need good analytical skills. It's a paradox that despite more data being available, we still find it problematic to measure the true impact of a change. At the start of any programme, we need to confirm what data is already available and which is to be acquired. We won't know whether we have achieved the goals and desired outcomes unless we have the relevant metrics. We may use experience and gut feeling to have an informed opinion, but nothing proves it like numbers. This chapter will cover why we don't measure change well enough and how to improve, and create a data-driven culture.

If you have no measures, did it even happen?

The most useful criteria to evaluate data is whether it's accurate and relevant. Not all data is equal, and it is open to interpretation. There is truth in Ronald Case's quote, 'Torture the data, and it will confess to anything.' Numbers are not as objective as we may think, and they can be used to prove whatever point one wants to make.

The contribution of change management activities is more complicated to disentangle from other transformation elements and more complex to measure because of intangible emotional reactions. The overall impact of automating a process can be easily measured, but how much of the cost savings was due to behavioural interventions facilitating employee adoption?

Metrics measuring the progress of a change programme are inputs for making timely adjustments. A company has its unique ecosystem, and people may not react as planned, so an intervention with all the hallmarks of success may not work. This is particularly true of multinational and cross-functional programmes, interventions and communications that bring excellent results in one country but are ineffective in another. Metrics allow us to understand what works well and give us the ability to tweak and adapt our approach.

Good data means good decisions. The challenge is finding the accurate and relevant data the business needs; the risk is using measures just because they are easy to gather. These vanity metrics may make us look good, but they don't give real value.

These are three essentials to measure change impacts.

Identify gaps

One of the most essential change deliverables is the change impact assessment (CIA), which shows the gap between the future and current state. It is an in-depth comparison between the present ways of working – including processes, skills and any legacy quirks – and the planned future. It determines the level of impact on multiple audiences. This level of granularity is required to keep the interventions focused and measure impacts more accurately.

I learnt this from an early project when I marked an impact as a medium across the board and realised too late that it was, in fact, high and disruptive for some of the teams.

Not every project needs a detailed assessment. The CIA gives insight into where we can expect greater resistance and uncover hidden operational inefficiencies. Impact data will inform the change interventions, prepare the company for the change, and be the precursor to assessing readiness for go-live.

Track progress

We need to track our progress as we work towards a future state. It's never too early to choose the right metrics for a reliable snapshot of people's work, productivity and behaviours before introducing any changes. Once a baseline is set, we can easily track progress over time.

I have worked on projects where the required data had never been – or wasn't consistently – collected. The sponsor initially believed that getting those metrics was too much effort and a distraction for the team. They had other priorities, and data collection could wait. Despite the time pressure, the counterargument was that the project team may be developing the wrong solution without the correct measures, which we would not know until too late, potentially wasting both time and effort. The compromise was a shorter set of metrics; they were the most useful ones, and they ensured the correct solution.

Bring focus

Regular metrics review allows us to check progress and make precise interventions, thus saving resources. The risk is making assumptions and drawing conclusions that are not data-driven and starting unnecessary actions. The benefit of accurate and relevant data is to confirm whether activities are adding value and moving the programme forward. Challenging questions are essential; however, some of them can cause knee-jerk reactions, making executives question the programme. They can cause a flurry of activities that add minimal value but are a source of distraction.

Why we fail to measure

One of the purposes of change management interventions is to reduce uncertainty, and data is a means to achieve that. There are still reasons we fail to measure.

Different priorities: I worked with a FTSE100 company running a major system implementation. I wanted to measure the time and effort saved by the HR team and people managers using the new system; this was integral to demonstrating the value of the change programme. There was no 'before' implementation data, so there was no way to analyse the actual impact. I hoped to get useful data from the new system. Instead, we could only measure if people were accessing the new system, not what they were doing once there and for how long. None of the IT people I spoke with knew how to do this; they never considered there was a need – their only interest was to get the system up and running, not to find out how it was used. Here lies one of the significant issues: priorities are different. Any executive responsible for the ultimate choice of system and supplier should include the relevant measures in their requirements.

Procrastination: Some programme teams feel no rush to agree on metrics and believe it is acceptable to start measuring when a project is close to going live – or even once it goes live. Their rationale is a focus on the urgent rather than the important in the long term.

There has been a shift in the past few years, driven by boards wanting more details and reassurance on what the programme is expected to deliver, thus requesting current performance data and projections of future benefits. It is a positive shift; the next stage is using a cross-section of data to tell a story that resonates even more with executives. Just imagine the more significant impact of the message, 'In January we had x sales fulfilment rate and now in September the rate is 40% higher.' I know I would rather present this story than a number that shows neither trend nor improvement.

Psychological barriers: Data may put us in a bad light, highlighting current failures and missing targets. As seen in the section about people, anything to do with emotional responses will likely trigger the worst resistance. Newly collected data may show that teams are not performing well. Context is important as we should not apportion blame for something we could not previously measure; instead, we should set expectations of how performance will be measured in the future and the benefits of having useful data.

Examine which reason is causing the biggest impact and its root causes, then start addressing them, one at a time. This is painstaking but the only option.

Tracking success: Measures create confidence

This is an example of how measures must be targeted for the most relevant outcomes. I was managing a global SAP implementation in one of the countries. The first attempt had been abandoned the previous year, so this time it had to be completed without delays or it would jeopardise the whole programme. The CIA highlighted a culture of resistance and very low attendance to any training – information backed up by data from the learning and development team. Employees rarely attended scheduled training, arrived late or were distracted by mobile devices. In this SAP implementation, training was essential; the system was different from the current one, and there were process and organisational changes as well. We wanted to change the attitude towards learning, emphasising its importance and benefits for their personal development. People had to attend multiple sessions over six weeks, so building and maintaining their focus was necessary.

The key measures were assimilating the content and confidence in applying the learning to use the system correctly. Actual attendance is usually easy to measure and done after the courses, but in this case, we needed a better option: track it even before the training sessions started.

We decided to leverage the hierarchical national culture in this Middle Eastern country. We set up the usual reminders to calendar invites, but most importantly, invites were sent for a time fifteen minutes in advance of the actual start. If the individual was not there, we would call them. If they didn't arrive after five minutes, we would call the manager. If still not there, we would go and look for the individual in the office. We arranged for free food before the training session – another incentive that became quickly known and contributed to getting people in early. We also had a box for people to leave their mobile phones in before entering the classroom.

It sounds draconian, and I would never use this approach in other companies or countries, but it was the best solution in this case. We achieved an attendance rate of 92%.

Not everything counts: Measuring what matters most

What to measure

The desired outcomes drive the choice of measures. Having extolled the virtues of measurements, it's important to remember there is a cost in terms of both time and resources. Let's focus on selecting the most useful rather than the merely interesting or 'just because they are available' metrics. We need a mix of quantitative and qualitative measures; since change is an emotional experience, it's essential to know how people feel about it. Metrics can drive the wrong behaviours (see my call centre experience in Chapter 4), so test scenarios to check if the new measures create unwelcome results.

- **Adoption.** We want to know this: 'Are people doing things differently?' Ideally, there are multiple data points, including adopting the new system, processes and behaviours. Because it takes time for new habits to become embedded, we need to track adoption over time to ensure sustainable change. My default is one month after go-live and then every quarter. The real benefits for the business start to become apparent after several months.

- **Productivity.** Employees may adopt the change, but are they more productive? Depending on the type of change, several data points can be used for a before and after comparison. One improvement is in the speed of completing an activity and removing administrative tasks.

My first projects were about improving the customer experience by making internal processes more efficient, such as reducing order fulfilment time, with a demonstrable improvement in productivity. Other situations are less straightforward; for example, we may reduce the time an HR person spends on admin tasks, but the real productivity depends on what they do with the saved time

- **Financial.** Seeking revenue increase, but especially cost reduction, drives most change programmes. The correct metrics are not always obvious. A programme may increase costs in a particular unit but decrease them overall – using the wrong metrics can lead to the wrong decisions. Chosen measures need to be tested to confirm they are useful and accurate, as does measuring over time. Benefits and savings aren't realised at go-live. It takes time for the new ways of working to become embedded, especially for complex changes.

This image illustrates how we can develop a framework of useful and relevant measures.

		When		
		At the start	During	Post implementation
What	People			
	Process			
	Systems			

A framework of measures

Sustainable adoption takes time, so we must take consistent measures after the programme is completed to ensure new habits are embedded.

How to measure

The chosen method needs to be consistent so as to enable tracking over time.

- **Before and after.** This is the most useful and easy to collect. The clue is in the words: a set of measures is taken as early as possible to provide a baseline. Measures are then taken at regular intervals. It's reliable and collects data consistently over time. Presenting this data at board or steering committees shows progress and draws attention to any areas of risk to enable effective decision-making.

- **Pilot and testing.** Sometimes, it's useful to start the project in a team or region to test impacts. This is a safe option because of the lower investment required and it gives the opportunity to modify future change interventions, communications and training. As shown in Chapter 5, success in one location does not imply that the same interventions will be successful everywhere else.

Two nuggets of insight from the study of human behaviours:

1. **Stated vs revealed preferences.** I discovered this during my social science research: people often don't mean what they tell you. Why? We want to present our better selves, prove we are smarter and more considerate, and choose what we believe others want to hear. For example, you may ask employees to choose between in-person learning and self-learning as their preferred training method. They state a preference for face-to-face training, probably because it is something they recognise, that gives direct access to trainers, or they see it as a company perk. Once the training is ready, rooms or online sessions are booked and invites are sent, employees don't attend, revealing their true preference for self-learning. Surveys are useful but shouldn't be relied upon. Trend data and observations are more reliable.

2. **Ask questions about what others do.** In addition to asking people about their personal experiences and opinions of the change, ask them questions about how their colleagues perceive the change and whether they are adopting the new system or ways of working. These questions give more accurate and truthful information since we are better observers of others and less likely to attach emotions to our response, i.e. we may not want

to admit we have ignored the new process and continued using our informal channels to get things done.

Accurate and reliable data is the start; it needs interpretation and, therefore, analytical skills. I once thought numbers don't lie, but then I learnt about statistical significance and outliers. We need to be sceptical and go beyond the headline numbers. Companies need employees who know how to interpret data.

A project ends but measuring never does

Programmes lose steam once they go live, especially long-term ones. People used to the cadence of project work want to move on and start something new. Without a business-as-usual owner and an effective handover, the hard work of many months or years can be wasted. Without regular checkpoints and measures, employees may not adopt or take full advantage of the change (i.e. features of the new system), and slowly revert to old habits. The outcome is no savings or productivity improvements. The solution is to incorporate measures into regular operations. It includes creating feedback loops through which employees can report what's working and what's not.

Continuous improvement and post-project ownership

Sustainable change requires a culture open to progress and future transformation.

A culture of continuous improvement means the intention to improve things is ingrained in employees' subconscious. They proactively use a change as a springboard for ideas and tweaks that make a system, process or activity even more effective. Some companies have successfully created this cultural trait. Toyota is one of the most famous and enduring examples. Every employee, from assembly line to top executive, is responsible for enhancing efficiency, quality and productivity. This culture of continuous improvement, known as kaizen, made Toyota an innovation leader, incorporating automation, AI and sustainability into its production processes. Another approach is to give employees time to explore ideas and projects outside of their primary job; companies such as 3M and Google use this approach as part of their drive to promote experimentation, an incubator of creative thinking and product development.

Summary

- Measuring the contribution of change management activities in a bigger programme is complex because it is linked to intangible emotional reactions. We need to improve measures of causation between behavioural interventions and employee adoption.

- We measure impacts and progress by identifying the gaps between the present and the future, determining the most appropriate interventions based on areas of potential resistance. We regularly check and adjust. Keeping metrics at the forefront of executive conversations brings focus to data-driven actions and decisions, which contributes to a cultural shift that ripples through the organisation.

- Among the reasons we fail to measure are different priorities, procrastination, and psychological barriers – normally a blend of the three.

- The choice of measures is driven by the desired outcomes, so we need to focus on useful rather than merely interesting or available data. The most relevant metrics from a change management perspective are adoption, productivity and financial.

- The measure method needs to be consistent so that change progress can be tracked over time. Before and after measurements are the most useful and easy to collect. Starting small with a pilot to test the change intervention allows us to learn and adapt in advance of the bigger programme.

- People may unintentionally mislead us by giving their stated preferences while their revealed ones remain hidden, as we want to present our better selves or say what we believe others want to hear. Be cautious of surveys, challenge the results and observe behaviours, where possible.

- Ask employees what they believe their colleagues' behaviours to be. People tend to be more observant of others and less likely to attach emotions to their response.

- Sustainable change requires a culture of continuous improvement and post-project ownership. This culture of improving things becomes ingrained in the subconscious of employees, who proactively want to improve their ways of working. Ownership is important to keep momentum, reap the long-term benefits, and prevent employees from slowly reverting back to the old ways of working.

EIGHT

Building A Culture Of Change Resilience

W e have explored opportunities to improve how executives lead and influence change in their organisations, from setting the direction to recognising blind spots via resistance, behaviours and culture. We are now ready for the last chapter, which includes a final round of lessons on ownership, planning fallacy and why letting go of a programme may be the best option.

The solutions include capabilities to develop change sustainability, a mindset of growth and resilience, and a tool to challenge the programme even before we start the change.

Avoiding accountability is a recipe for disaster

Some projects have roles with no clear accountability, or people are asked to fulfil multiple roles because of a lack of resources, thus making it hard to have solid governance.

I remember a project with no official process owners. Several experts developed the new workflows and contributed to the CIA; however, there was no accountable owner during the programme or post-go-live. The board acknowledged the issue, but the decision was delayed and nobody was appointed. We communicated the purpose of the change and trained employees, but without a process owner driving the message, there was no traction for a sustainable change. As a result, the initial improvements and adherence to the new processes soon fizzled out.

The following are signs of accountability gaps:

- **Confusion about roles.** Uncertainty about who is responsible for what leads to duplication and actions not being taken. Be wary of RACI (Responsible, Accountable, Consulted, Informed) as the solution. Although popular, it is too simplistic to map people to activities using this model as it doesn't capture the complexity of

many projects, lacks flexibility and gets quickly
outdated.

- **Slow or no decisions.** This tends to happen if the
  sponsor or senior stakeholders change. Without
  a clear owner, decisions are delayed as nobody
  believes they have the authority to proceed.
  Even if responsibility is delegated, there is still a
  reluctance to formally accept it.

- **No-shows.** That's how I refer to people unwilling
  to assume ownership, either because they believe
  they should not be accountable or they may
  fear failure, or the change involves multiple
  departments and they are not prepared to take
  responsibility. In any of these situations, there is
  limited progress.

The most significant impacts are on decision-making
and progress. Here are some solutions:

- **Clear governance structure.** This must be the
  first action when setting up a programme,
  but it should not be seen as a one-off exercise.
  Instead, it must be regularly revised and
  consistently referred to. Balance is required
  between a comprehensive governance covering
  structure, roles and how decisions are made and
  maintaining the flexibility to respond to rising
  risks and issues.

- **Accountability by outcomes.** Rather than using a RACI, which is a static document, make people accountable for outcomes and deliverables. It puts a much stronger emphasis on ownership and encourages people towards greater collaboration.

- **A culture that encourages accountability.** A corporate culture that supports accountability will naturally ensure the most appropriate governance and frameworks are created and used. The expression 'most appropriate' is essential. Structures have to be based on the type and size of the company to be effective; if they are too cumbersome they won't be followed.

Planning fallacy, or why everything always takes longer than we think

This cognitive bias is so common that even the person who identified it fell for it...

Daniel Kahneman, the late Nobel prize winner and author of *Thinking, Fast and Slow*, tells a personal story of him and a group of colleagues writing a new curriculum and textbook for high school students.[43] The topic was judgement and decision-making, their area

---

43   D Kahneman, *Thinking Fast and Slow* (Penguin, 2011), p. 245

of expertise, and they estimated two years to complete. After one year, they convened to review their progress and confirm the completion date. Kahneman decided to use one of the techniques in the planned textbook and asked each member to confidentially write their estimate, which consistently came around the two-year mark. He then had an idea and asked one of his colleagues how long similar teams took to complete similar projects. Nobody in the group had considered that question. It came as a shock to everybody when the colleague replied that 40% failed to complete the task, and it took the others seven to ten years to complete it. Despite the evidence, the incredible thing is that they did not quit that day. It took eight years to complete the curriculum and book, which were never used.

Psychologists Daniel Kahneman and Amos Tversky first identified the planning fallacy in 1979. This bias explains how people tend to underestimate the time, costs and risks associated with a task, even when they have actual data from previous experiences. Kahneman referred to the behaviour in the example above as 'irrational perseverance'. We can all relate to instances when, facing a choice, we give up rationality rather than the goal.

Sounds familiar? This is what it looks like in a project:

- **Optimistic time estimates.** We believe we can complete activities faster than is realistic. It applies to anything from writing a report, building the space shuttle or renovating your home. Similarly to Kahneman and his colleagues, we come up with a time that is either a round figure, linked to an event (e.g. before summer) or feels right – there is no rationality to the estimate.

- **Ignore past experience.** We tend to ignore any evidence of our own past experiences or from other cases. Even highly experienced programme managers disregard the actual data and instead anchor their timelines to past plans, despite knowing they were delayed. We assume we can do it better or faster this time.

- **Focus on the ideal outcome.** We set a deadline based on what we wish to happen, e.g. wouldn't it be nice to be in the new home by Christmas? (No matter if you just laid the foundations in June.) We overlook potential risks and unforeseen events in our plans. We also suspect that a realistic estimate of time and cost may prevent the board from approving the programme.

Sometimes, it's useful to play the role of the negative person in a meeting.

My experience: The value of sceptics

I am an optimist; however, I recognise the need to play the opposite character. It was never more necessary than in a project with a small, forward-looking company. The weekly board meetings were full of ideas and enthusiasm; nothing was ever impossible and optimism permeated the room. This is not something I am used to.

I embraced the positive vibes initially – it was fun and infectious – but then something started nagging at me. I thought the team was overcommitting and some dates were overly optimistic. I knew I could not simply disagree, even if my opinion was substantiated by evidence, as it would have created a barrier between us and possibly an outright rejection of my opinions. Instead, I positioned it as, 'Let me play the role of…'. This would range from acting as a product manager not receiving a prototype for another month or as a marketing manager not having access to the edited videos from the agency in time.

This more subtle approach was useful to introduce the possibility of something going wrong – just a pinch of negativeness in this enthusiastic team. My objective was to prompt either the realisation that action was required to prevent a risk from happening or to adjust the timescales. After the initial and instinctive resistance among the board members, the role play shifted the attitude towards a more realistic and pragmatic approach.

Overcoming planning fallacy

Planning fallacy easily sneaks into most projects, and that's why the reality of projects is different from how we envisage them.

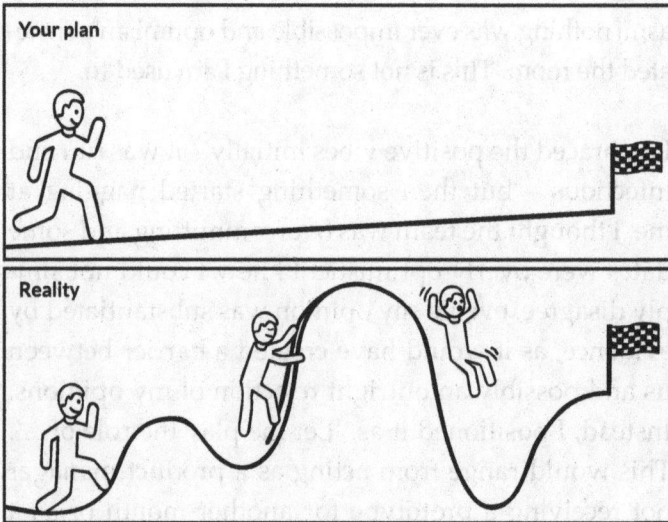

Planning fallacy

Knowing planning fallacy exists should make it easier to avoid. Here are some techniques:

- **Use historical data.** It's unlikely a project is unique, and there is bound to be information on cost, timescale and resource requirements about similar ones. Be realistic and don't expect anything of note to get done during festivities and holiday periods. Pesky events such as the financial calendar also dictate periods when progress is on hold.

- **Build the plan from the bottom up.** Often, we set a date for the future (based on over-optimism or because it makes us look good) and retrofit the activities. Plan in reverse, starting with the main activities, estimating duration and working out the end date. I decided to try this method when writing this book. I started writing most days for two weeks and averaged the number of words per day, which was the foundation for estimating the timescale of writing the first draft version. I then planned half as much time to have a (proper) draft that I could submit for appraisal. That's when I realised that 'it would be nice to have it done in four months' was overly optimistic.

- **Include buffers, but not too many.** One of the risks of building a plan from the bottom up is that contributors suddenly become cautious and add extra days to each activity. The problem is that those extra days scattered across a plan add up to long timescales; they make the project unrealistic and may cause it to be rejected. Adding extra time is necessary because of unforeseen obstacles and delays, but it needs to be balanced and realistic.

- **Have the plan critiqued.** Share the purpose of your programme and plan with others in the organisation, asking them to act as devil's advocate. Most people are overly nice and withdraw from direct feedback, so you may need to clearly demand they pull it apart. And – most importantly – listen to them.

- **Be truthful with your sponsor and board.**
There is pressure to get things done quickly, achieve significant increases in revenues and decrease costs. Seeking financial approval for a programme that lasts several years is not easy; however, seeking approval for more money and time halfway through is not ideal either. Splitting the programme into phases simplifies gaining support and allows the board to appraise progress at the end of each phase. If you have removed as much planning fallacy as possible, you will present a programme that progresses on time and within budget.

Allocating planning time at the programme's start will save time and money later on.

When giants stumble: Lessons from corporate missteps

We may think that some companies always get it right, so it's good to remember that even prominent brand names make false steps sometimes.

EXAMPLE: Apple – not getting it right every time

Apple launched the Newton Personal Digital Assistant in 1993, but it was a commercial failure.[44] The concept was innovative but expensive and unreliable, and the device was bulky. It was discontinued a few years later with heavy financial losses. Apple Maps in 2012 was also imbued with inaccurate information and poor navigation, attracting strong criticism.[45]

EXAMPLE: Blockbuster's billion-dollar buyout refusal

Back in 2000, Blockbuster, who dominated the movie rental business with its brick-and-mortar shops worldwide, was approached by a small company called Netflix, specialising in DVD rentals by mail. They were open to be bought with a price tag of $50 million.[46] Blockbuster turned them down, believing it was a niche market with no future. Netflix is now worth billions.

44 L Dormehl, 'Today in Apple History: Steve Jobs Flip-Flops on the Newton', *Cult of Mac* (4 September 2024), www.cultofmac.com/news/apple-history-steve-jobs-kills-newton, accessed 4 April 2025

45 R Cellan-Jones, 'New Apple Maps App Under Fire from Users', *BBC News* (20 September 2012), www.bbc.co.uk/news/technology-19659736, accessed 4 April 2025

46 J Dalton and A Logan, 'Lessons from the Rise of Netflix and the Fall of Blockbuster', *CATO Institute* (26 October 2024), www.cato.org/commentary/lessons-rise-netflix-fall-blockbuster, accessed 4 April 2025

There are many other cases. The lesson is about noticing the red flags soon enough to avoid development costs and a product with no market.

The importance of knowing when to walk away

One of the most contentious decisions in any programme is to stop it. Why is this so hard, even if both data and our gut instinct tell us it is the best option? An executive with a stake in a major programme fears their reputation will be tagged with the programme being axed. Unsurprisingly, many of the reasons are emotional:

- **Escalation of commitment.** The more committed we are to a decision, the more difficult it is to stop, even when the evidence is clear that neither the desired outcome nor the planned benefits will be achieved. The commitment already made creates a vicious cycle that makes stopping increasingly difficult. The problem is more marked with programmes spanning departments with conflicting priorities and multiple decision-makers.

- **Sunk cost fallacy.** Having invested significant time and money in a project makes it hard to stop. The need to continue in the hope of recovering the investment is compelling. Even if we rationally know that we cannot recover those costs, there is still an emotional attachment and we don't want to see resources wasted. We fail to consider the additional cost of investing in the failing project and, conversely, the gains of investing in a new solution.

- **Optimism bias.** We pin our hopes that 'something' will turn around a failing project. This magic intervention may be a new leader joining, better skilled resources or increased investment. We ignore the visible evidence that the project is unlikely to improve.

I remember talking with a senior executive about a programme to digitalise the customer and internal platform. The programme was running three years late, and by now, the solution was out of date in both looks and functionality. Despite this knowledge, the hope that the project would deliver the desired solution was still high, as was the reluctance to let go.

It may seem gloomy, but this is an opportunity to change our attitude. Shift the thinking from 'once started, can't stop' to 'what's the best investment choice?' Stopping one programme and allocating resources to another may be the best option for the company's long-term success.

Reframing the situation

Here, I am sharing some solutions that revolve around reframing the situation, which has the advantage of managing the emotional part of difficult decisions if the data already demonstrates that the project should stop.

- **Emphasise the gains.** Reframe the programme assessment to emphasise future costs and benefits rather than past investment (sunk costs), and consider what you can gain rather than what you have lost. We naturally tend to prefer avoiding losses over acquiring equivalent gains. Scenario analysis is a valuable tool for visualising options and ensuring decisions are data-driven.

- **Seek an external view.** It's easy to get caught up with optimism bias and team groupthink, so we must regularly seek an unbiased external perspective on the programme's progress and feasibility. External opinions are key here; people connected with the programme will carry similar biases, and since they are already involved, they will be reluctant to stop it. The ideal external view is comparable to a non-exec board. Including regular checkpoints as milestones in the plan ensures they are prioritised.

- **Have an exit strategy.** Although it should be part of most programmes, it rarely is, which I blame on optimism bias and overconfidence. Who wants to spend time at the start of a project to consider the circumstances under which you would stop it? It is the best time to create a structured approach to winding down a failing project, with less political, logistical and emotional friction. Setting up an exit strategy and performing a pre-mortem (see later in this chapter) are some of the most counter-intuitive and innovative techniques in any executive toolbox.

Letting go may be hard, but it can be the best decision in the long run.

My experience: Change can be good for you

I was on my first job after university, starting a career in procurement. I was a buyer in the energy department, working with a senior buyer and reporting to a more experienced senior buyer. I got to meet suppliers, but I was mainly helping these two managers.

After three months, they announced a reorganisation of the whole procurement function. I didn't know what reorganisation meant until a senior manager called me into his office and told me he was the new head of the department for energy and facilities procurement and I would be reporting to him. The two senior buyers moved to other roles.

My initial reaction was shock. Four months into the job, I was suddenly responsible for placing contracts and managing suppliers – not even small ones; these were the biggest oil companies in the world, with contracts worth millions of pounds per year. The shock was replaced by excitement. It was a great opportunity that I took full advantage of. My first experience as a recipient of change has probably biased my views; I saw and still see change as an opportunity rather than something to fight against. Since I started working as a change manager, I have aimed to instil this perspective in the people I work with.

Learning to embrace change

Change is inevitable. Even if we resist, it's going to happen anyway so we may as well take advantage of it. This works both ways. It is the leaders' responsibility to be fair and open about what the change entails and support employees in the journey.

Embedding change is the means to achieve the desired outcomes and benefits. It can be a fraught experience. Executives may get frustrated if employees are not adopting the change or are slowly reverting to the old ways of doing things. Employees complain that the frequency of changes does not allow them to settle and do their jobs. Who is right? Both. It may seem like change is something we fight against, but embracing it as a learning perspective can become a positive experience.

Creating a sustainable change culture

Here is some advice on how to create a sustainable change culture.

- **Embed change.** Make it an element of the culture, where it's accepted as part of the normal flow. For example, if there are frequent reorganisations, position it as an opportunity and make this part of the company's fabric. This knowledge can inspire employees to engage in more collaborative behaviours since they know they may one day work closely with people who are now in other departments or countries, encouraging them to forge good relationships.

- **Measure adoption.** We covered this in Chapter 6; however, it is good to remember that if people know adoption and adherence will be measured, they are more likely to make it a priority. Because we tend to follow what our colleagues do (remember the social norms), these new positive habits are going to spread more easily and become the new way of working.

- **Leadership role modelling.** Employees are more likely to follow if leaders visibly support the change (in action rather than words).

- **Build capabilities.** We can't expect managers to build support for change within their teams if they don't have knowledge of managing people's change journeys. This is more than just training; it requires recognising the importance of employee morale, the investment in learning and optimal management practices.

- **Recognise and reward success.** I know of only one company that had a line item in the project plan called 'Celebrate success'. It was a big party a month after go-live, and even the people who were involved in the early stages of the project were invited. I encourage every project manager to include celebration time.

Sustainability in how we implement change can be a competitive advantage in the marketplace. Change happens in every company, so let's improve how we do it.

The best time to spot failure? Before it happens

We are familiar with the concept of a post-mortem: scrutinising what went wrong after an event, but by then it's too late. What if we had a tool to prevent things from going wrong?

Spotting failure before it happens – or pre-mortem – is a powerful tool that can benefit any major programme. I came across it while studying behavioural science and liked it so much that I centred my thesis on it. It has profound influences, as Kahneman reflected after mentioning the idea of pre-mortem at a session in Davos: 'Someone behind me muttered, "It was worth coming to Davos just for this!" I later noticed that the speaker was the CEO of a major international corporation.'[47]

A pre-mortem is used within a group to evaluate a plan or a business decision. It is designed to remove bias and emotions and encourage participants to have an open discussion.

The simplicity of pre-mortem belies its power. Once you have an agreed purpose and plan, you gather the sponsor, programme team and other key stakeholders in a meeting. You set the scene: ask them to imagine they are one year (or any date) ahead in the future and the project has failed disastrously. You then ask them to write what may have gone wrong individually. I tend to give them 20 to 30 minutes (you want people to go beyond the easy answers that first come to mind and get into the more creative part of their brains). We then read and discuss each of them in turn.

---

47   D Kahneman, *Thinking Fast and Slow* (Penguin, 2011), p. 264

What has gone wrong?	Any inputs welcome	Finding themes and patterns	Taking action

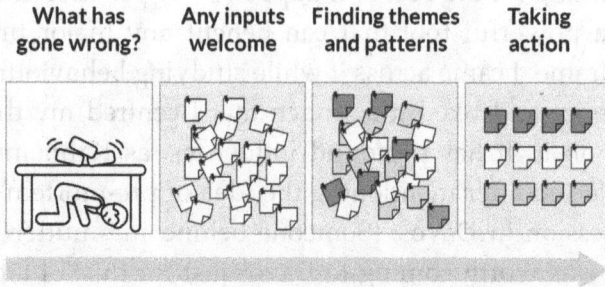

Pre-mortem

The benefits of this technique are:

- **It is practical and straightforward.** Project failure is presented as a fact that reframes how we perceive events. When the question is 'What *could* go wrong?' our brain seeks a hypothesis that defends the preparation work and we fear we may have to restart it. If we state something has already happened and ask 'What *has* gone wrong?' then our brain seeks reasons without as much emotional baggage.

- **It frees up the mind.** By stating the project has failed, people relax and their minds become more curious. It encourages people to come up with left-field reasons, which is the benefit of the exercise: moving away from the expected towards something that has not been considered before and can be most valuable, be it new ideas or alternative scenarios.

- **It breaks away from the norm.** Some of the reasons that come up would never emerge from a 'normal' programme risk assessment. For example, a CEO's retirement may cause the failure of a million pounds environmental sustainability programme or a significant system deployment failing because people working in the field don't have compatible portable devices.

- **There is no social pressure.** People are not asked to criticise their own or their colleagues' or leaders' plans. It debiases the attachment people have towards a plan they have contributed to and can evaluate it from an external perspective. It avoids any critique that can affect the social identity of the group.

- **It is written rather than spoken.** Writing down reasons for failure facilitates contributions from people who fear speaking in public – often more junior employees or subject matter experts. It also reduces the influence of dominant personalities by giving everybody the space to write their thoughts in silence.

People may worry that the pre-mortem exercise will lead to not starting, delaying or modifying projects. This must be seen as a positive outcome, as it highlights that some projects may not be viable or profitable. The more likely outcome is an improved strategy and execution.

The pre-mortem technique requires respecting the following rules:

- Make it a stand-alone activity, and the only activity planned for that day. Don't attach it to another meeting or it will lose its power.

- Purpose and plan must be completed first to have something tangible to critique.

- Scene setting is critical to get into the right mindset. It works best when out of the office.

- Use an external person to facilitate the discussion.

- Have a range of roles and expertise present. Diversity gives essential alternative perspectives.

Leaders developing the right attitude towards change

A change-embracing culture is progressive and innovative. Its people are resilient and don't let short-term setbacks stop long-term growth. How do you create this change-embracing culture?

The book *Mindset* by Carol Dweck lays the foundations for developing a positive attitude towards making mistakes and learning from them.[48]

The following are some building blocks:

- **Encourage learning and personal development.**
  This is skewed towards so-called 'soft' skills.
  Technical skills are important and easier to
  learn; it takes a lot of practice to become more
  emotionally intelligent. The basis of personal
  development is self-awareness and the grit
  to keep going, even when you don't see any
  progress. Consider learning as a holistic
  experience which goes beyond attending a
  course. The role of the leader is to encourage
  employees to see change as an opportunity
  to learn new skills and one which offers
  development possibilities. It can include
  time within the working week dedicated to
  development or to practise and innovate.

- **Normalise failure.** I worked in a company
  where the language was centred on blame and
  looking for the culprit. Employees worried
  about the consequences of getting something
  wrong won't take the initiative and default to
  the minimum effort. This is the opposite of a
  growth culture. We learn from mistakes: our own

48 C Dweck, *Mindset: Changing the way you think to fulfil your potential* (Robinson, 2017)

and others. Encourage people to come forward quickly if they believe something is not right. The role of the leader is to encourage people to experiment, take calculated risks and ensure there is a learning process. When people embrace challenges, they are more likely to overachieve.

- **Growth-oriented feedback.** Feedback looks easy but is hard to do in practice. Some managers are excellent, others avoid it (especially if they feel uncomfortable with conflict) and most muddle through. Feedback is not about pointing out weaknesses. Instead, it is about using the conversation as an opportunity for growth. The emphasis is on 'how we did something' rather than 'what happened', and the objective is to promote effort and improvement, as well as recognise and reward progress. It is for leaders to learn how to best give feedback and then model these behaviours to become routine across the organisation.

- **Resilience.** In a culture of resilience, people adapt to changes, recover from setbacks and thrive in uncertainty. This is rarely the case, so we must develop this culture, characterised by adaptability and realising that change is the means of progress. The role of leadership is to develop resilience by empowering people, communicating clearly and openly, and ensuring emotional support, if individuals and teams need it.

- **'Fail fast, learn faster'.** Facebook's motto until 2014 was 'Move fast and break things'. I agree with the emphasis on speed but I never liked breaking things. It feels like an excuse to be disruptive for the sake of it, especially if we don't provide a valuable alternative and end up breaking valuable things. I prefer, 'Fail fast, learn faster'.

Summary

- Without clear accountability, we experience slow or no decisions, confusion about roles and a lack of ownership. The outcome is a lack of progress or not achieving the programme goals. The solution is a clear governance structure and a culture that encourages accountability.

- Planning fallacy is a bias explaining how we tend to underestimate the time, costs and risks associated with a task, even when we have actual data proving the error. Solve it by relying on data to set realistic expectations based on similar ones. Be clear about how long activities on the critical path will take; include buffers, but not too many. Strike a balance between expecting delays and being too risk-averse; and seek external critique of the plan.

- Teams – especially the most positive and enthusiastic ones – need a naysayer to bring a realistic and pragmatic view. This can be a thankless role, so position it as 'Let me play the role of…' to raise challenging questions or risks.

- Stopping a programme is a contentious decision. Even when all the data supports it, emotional reasons still make it hard to stop it. The three most relevant reactions are escalation of commitment, sunk cost fallacy and optimism bias. Shifting our perception from 'Once started, can't stop' to 'What's the best investment choice?' can help us stop a programme and allocate resources to a project with higher returns. Solutions include reframing, getting an external view and having an exit strategy.

- If we embrace change as a learning perspective, it can become a positive experience. We need to create a culture of sustainable change, which includes accepting change as the normal state and clearly positioning its benefits to employees.

- The pre-mortem is a technique used to evaluate a plan or a business decision, designed to remove bias and emotions. We benefit by reframing our perception of events with curiosity rather than defensiveness. The outcome is an alternative set of more profound reasons that don't emerge from a simple assessment.

- A change-embracing culture is progressive and innovative. People are resilient and don't let short-term setbacks stop long-term growth. The building blocks to developing this culture are encouraging learning and personal development, normalising failure, and growth-oriented feedback to develop resilience.

Conclusion

Change is inevitable, but *successful* change is not. We have explored the many layers that contribute to the success or failure of change programmes, from leadership blind spots to creating a resilient corporate culture that adopts change more readily. Let's reflect on the key lessons and what they mean in practice for leaders inside the change maze.

Reactions to change

Change is fundamentally about people and is an emotional experience; thus, explaining it with data and facts doesn't work. We are driven by emotions, biases, habits and deeply ingrained cultural norms. This applies at board level as well as on the shop floor. The best-planned transformation that doesn't consider this is at risk of failure.

The perspective and experience of change differ between leaders and employees impacted by the change. Leaders may have spent months designing a strategy and case for change and have internalised what the change means for them and the business. Therefore, they assume that employees will understand it instantly. Employees need the time to move along the change curve, making sense of the change and what it means for them.

We interpret messages through our filters, biases and personal experiences. What seems obvious to one person can be utterly opaque to another. Messages need repetition, building on the level of detail over time. Communication must be refined and tested, and feedback must be actively sought to ensure understanding. Also dangerous is to expect that a change approach that has been successful in the past or a region will work again without modification.

Change triggers emotional responses, and resistance should not be seen as an obstacle but as a source of insight. Employees' pushback arises from real concerns such as fear of the unknown, loss of control or threat to competence. They must be addressed by acknowledging these fears and providing clear, meaningful responses. Even if correct, logical explanations of efficiency gains won't reassure someone who fears their job is at risk. People change when they see value in the new ways of working, not because they are forced to.

Change management programmes

Change management is not a checklist of plans, impact assessments, communications and training sessions. It requires flexibility, trialling interventions, testing and tweaking. Always remember that people embrace change when they understand its purpose and what it means for them, and when they see those around them committing to the new way of working and feel safe in the new working environment.

Change programmes fail to achieve the desired benefits without emphasising adoption and measuring progress over time. Go-live is an important date, but success and the real benefits are achieved after implementation, through productivity increases and cost savings, as new systems, processes and operating models become embedded. A baseline needs to be set at the programme's start, tracking the right metrics and using them to make any adjustments. Monitoring adoption, productivity and financial impact continuously will sustain momentum beyond the initial excitement.

The impact of culture on change

Culture is the ever-present but invisible force that shapes everything in a company. A culture centred on stability and a shared sense of purpose will help employees navigate uncertainty. Culture is present at multiple levels – national, corporate and functional – and all play a part in a successful change. A cultural shift is complex and takes time; however, tweaks that introduce new habits, rituals and stories are consistently reinforced over time, and achieve tangible and positive shifts.

The leadership role in change

For senior executives, the ability to lead change is a strategic imperative. Nothing is still in business: technologies advance at a breakneck pace, markets evolve, new competitors appear suddenly on the horizon and customer expectations shift with the latest influencer whim. Despite decades of change, organisations still make the same mistakes.

Misalignment between a change programme and overall strategy, or conflict between programmes, can derail the best-laid plans. Short-term fixes that contradict long-term direction, tensions between central decisions and local realities, and conflicting team priorities contribute to wasted resources, declining morale and a loss of credibility. Leaders must ensure suitable governance structures are in place to support the change, and decision-making is informed by data.

The leaders' role is to look forward, but the risk is getting trapped in a bubble, disconnected from operational realities. This may become a problem in companies where only good news travels upwards, and critical issues are unnoticed until they suddenly become a crisis. Such a culture may develop unknowingly over time; therefore, a concerted effort is required to promote transparency and value diverse perspectives, exposing blind spots before they become issues. A change of course should be considered a sign of strength, not failure.

Leading change is a role that never ends. Companies exist in a state of continuous adaptation, so developing resilience and a culture accepting of change is crucial. The most effective leaders embrace this reality and recognise their role in creating an environment where change is seen as normal, expected and maybe even welcomed by employees as an opportunity. Change is a journey.

Acknowledgements

There are many people I have met and worked with in the past twenty years, and they have all contributed in varying degrees to the making of this book. Each project contributed to my knowledge of business and the intricacies of change, from designing a strategy to implementing new systems. I have learnt about cultural diversity from living and working in different countries and from conversations with people from so many other countries worldwide. Thank you to the executives who shared their views and experiences of change in conversations and interviews. I worked with hundreds of people – too many to name here – therefore, I chose to say a massive thank you rather than risk missing someone out.

Many thanks to the academics and fellow students at the University of Bath and the London School of Economics for shaping my thinking on all business-related topics and opening the doors to many insights into human behaviour.

I want to give special thanks to the team at Rethink. Being my first book, I didn't realise how many components there are to get to publishing day. So, I am grateful for the guidance and for making it a great experience.

Thanks to family and friends for the ongoing support during the exciting and challenging times.

I have dedicated this book to my dad. He would never have imagined his daughter writing a book. I know he would be incredibly proud.

Finally, thank you in advance to the leaders and change-makers who read this book. If you have found even one nugget of insight or source of inspiration to make your change successful, then I have achieved my purpose.

The Author

Giorgia Prestento is an organisational transformation expert with more than twenty years' experience leading change programmes for high-profile global organisations. Throughout her career, she has collaborated with boards and leadership teams. Her hands-on experience across diverse industries enables her to offer actionable, real-world insights. Combining deep practical expertise with academic learning – she holds an MBA from the University of Bath School of Management and a master's in behavioural science from the London

School of Economics – allows her to effectively address the human factors that underpin successful transformations.

🌐 giorgiaprestento.com

🔗 www.linkedin.com/in/giorgiaprestento